Joe **MUST** Go.

Joe

MUST

Go

by Leroy Gore
Sauk City, Wisconsin

Julian Messner, Inc.   New York

Published by Julian Messner, Inc.
8 West 40th Street, New York 18

Published simultaneously in Canada
by The Copp Clark Company, Ltd.

Copyright 1954 by Leroy Gore
Printed in the United States of America

Library of Congress Catalog Card No. 54–12703

These pages are proudly dedicated to the 335,000 "little people" for their courage and decency and moral dignity— qualities too often sacrificed on the altar of political expediency by the "big people" and the United States Senate. If they had signed in their own blood, their signatures would be no better evidence of the staunchness of their hearts and the firmness of their souls.

Here is the essence of democracy, the well-defined proof for those who have eyes to see that the "big people" alone are too small to defend our democratic freedoms with their scant weapons of stubborn illusion; only the "little people" are big enough to face the consequences of disillusionment and conquer them, unafraid.

It is no biological accident that God has created so many "little people." The meek shall indeed inherit the earth, and it is well for the proud and the mighty that this is so.

From the

Wisconsin Constitution

ARTICLE XIII . . . *Section 12* . . . *"Recall of elective officers.*
The qualified electors of the state or of any county or of any
congressional, judicial or legislative district may petition for the
recall of any elective officer after the first year of the term for
which he was elected, by filing a petition with the officer with
whom the petition for nomination to such office in the primary
election is filed, demanding the recall of such officer. Such petition shall be signed by electors equal in number to at least
twenty-five percent of the vote cast for the office of governor at
the last preceding election, in the state, county or district from
which such officer is to be recalled. The officer with whom such
petition is filed shall call a special election to be held not less
than forty nor more than forty-five days from the filing of such

petition. The officer against whom such petition has been filed shall continue to perform the duties of his office until the result of such special election shall have been officially declared. Other candidates for such office may be nominated in the manner as is provided by law in primary elections. The candidate who shall receive the highest number of votes shall be deemed elected for the remainder of the term. The name of the candidate against whom the recall petition is filed shall go on the ticket unless he resigns within ten days after the filing of the petition. After one such petition and special election, no further recall petition shall be filed against the same officer during the term for which he was elected. This article shall be self-executing and all of its provisions shall be treated as mandatory. Laws may be enacted to facilitate its operation, but no law shall be enacted to hamper, restrict or impair the right of recall."

ARTICLE I . . . *Section 4* . . . *"Right to assemble and petition.* The right of the people peaceably to assemble, to consult for the common good, and *to petition the government,* or any department thereof, *shall never be abridged."*

FOREWORD

The newspaperman—particularly the small-town weekly editor —is in a fair way to being the conscience of Amercia. As the weekly publisher of the Sauk-Prairie *Star* in Sauk City, Wisconsin (population 1,755), Leroy Gore represents the average small-town weekly editor. He is a man of fifty who has moved around considerably in the Midwest. He was born and raised in Iowa, was graduated from the University of Nebraska journalism school in 1928, and served his journalistic apprenticeship on small newspapers in Iowa and Nebraska. He worked on newspapers in Fort Atkinson, Clintonville, and owned the Spring Valley, Wisconsin *Sun* before he came into Sauk City to begin a new weekly back in 1952.

He belongs to a healthy American tradition—that of Mark Twain and Will Rogers, of Ed Howe and William Allen White. He has a wry sense of humor, a placid nature, and a feeling for words. He seldom comes to a boil. It took him a long time to rebel against the junior senator from Wisconsin, but look what happened when at last he did!

It seems to us here that Sauk City, Wisconsin, was in a large sense the natural place for the rebellion against mccarthyism to begin. The town was founded by a Hungarian count with liberal leanings who got out of Europe just one leap ahead of Prince Metternich's police. It was settled by German '48ers who were in rebellion against the autocratic life they led in Bavaria and other provinces of the old Germany. Its cultural pattern was set by a strong nucleus of "Freethinkers," the offshoot of a Humanist movement begun at the University of Prague early in the nineteenth century, and this cultural pattern has dominated the village ever since 1838, when the first settler reached its site. Moreover, it became sensitive to politics early; almost to a man, the town fell in behind the sweeping liberal policies of the late great Robert M. LaFollette, Sr., at the turn of the century.

Sauk City is a town in which Catholic, Freethinker, and Protestant live amicably side by side. Occasionally it erupts into violent disagreements, chiefly verbal, but, come time to sit down to the next meal, the partisans of the most violent quarrels find it possible to sit down together.

Sauk City was a natural place for Leroy Gore to settle down. The trouble was, he couldn't stay settled. And often those restless people who find it hard to settle into a rut are those who spur the rest of us to actions we have been putting off too long. Mccarthyism was in need of a catalytic agent like Leroy Gore.

AUGUST DERLETH

Author of *Evening in Spring* and one hundred other books, mostly about Sauk-Prairie

Sauk City, Wisconsin
21 July 1954

This is the old, old story of the Evil Ism.

It began in the Garden of Eden where Adam and Eve pointed an accusing finger at a subversive snake, even though they shared his guilt.

The Evil Ism, not the poisoned cup, killed Socrates.

The Evil Ism killed Jesus Christ.

The Evil Ism may well destroy our young and floundering Democracy.

It is not difficult to detect the Evil Ism. It says: "You must give me the right to believe as I believe, but I won't give you the right to believe as you believe."

The Ku Klux Klan was an Ism.

Hitlerism was an Ism.

Communism is an Ism.

Mccarthyism is an Ism.

Joe **MUST** Go

THE CASE OF

THE UNCONVINCED

CORPSE...

It's bad manners and downright indecent for a corpse to argue with the undertaker at his own funeral.

Mccarthyism is dead. But unfortunately someone has done a sloppy job of embalming. In view of this distressing situation, the funeral rites may consume four painful years, and it is conceivable that during this period the unconvinced corpse may leap from his coffin to clobber the pallbearers unmercifully on frequent occasions.

Only the people—specifically the people of Wisconsin—can sign a speedy death certificate for mccarthyism and nail down the lid of the coffin.

The United States Senate can't do it. The administration

can't do it. Even the courts couldn't do it because a thrust at Senator McCarthy by any of these agencies would serve only to endow mccarthyism with martyrdom. Any of these agencies might topple Senator McCarthy from his throne, but they cannot destroy mccarthyism. Only the soul of the people, reflected in their signatures and their ballots, can kill an Evil Ism.

That is why the Wisconsin recall movement is the only weapon McCarthy and his apostles, firmly entrenched for four long years, really fear.

The frenzied disciples of McCarthy have a way of repealing laws and even portions of the Constitution without due process of law. By invective and distortion, by the vilification of witnesses who take refuge in it, they have effectively destroyed the Fifth Amendment to the Constitution of the United States. Given enough time, they can destroy the Bill of Rights and the Constitution itself paragraph by paragraph.

By ridicule and carefully planted distortion they have attempted to repeal and make ineffective Wisconsin's recall legislation. They have tried to make it appear that anyone who promotes and signs or circulates a recall petition has large holes in his head. They have laughed at the recall effort as impractical and unconstitutional in one deep breath. In the next breath they have made it clear that those who sign may be subjected to vague and frightful retaliations. They have made hundreds of less veiled threats of physical violence, arson, kidnaping, and murder. They have attempted to read out of the Republican party those lifelong Republicans who regard the recall as a moral issue, even though most of these Republicans have a longer and better record of party affiliation than the junior senator, who was once a noisy Democrat during the "Twenty Years of Treason," and deserted the Democratic party for noisy Republicanism only in the interests of selfish political expediency. They have lumped the virtuous Democrats who participate in the movement with "left-wingers and Communists."

In one breath they have giggled at the recall as a hopelessly amateurish effort, in the next they have labeled it as a dastardly, cleverly planned plot of potent and dangerous radicals. The first charge is undeniably true. The latter charge is a highly amusing falsehood.

If the Wisconsin recall is a symptom of holes in the head, those holes are undeniably in the heads of Wisconsin lawmakers who wrote the recall legislation two decades ago, and the Republican legislatures which have endorsed that legislation with each succeeding session. Wisconsin, cradle of constructive American liberalism, recognizes that the right to recall is as fundamental as the right to elect; the right to sign a petition is as precious as the right to cast a ballot.

You may make a note on your calendar right now: mccarthyism will be permanently and thoroughly buried early in 1955.

This is no reckless and prejudiced piece of propaganda. This is a political certainty, based upon the results of the initial recall effort.

More than 400,000 Wisconsin citizens have signed recall petitions. Some of them signed too early, some signed too late. Some committed innocently technical blunders. But more than a third of a million qualified electors of the state signed properly notarized petitions within the legal sixty-day limit provided by law.

If this be failure, surely it is the most successful failure in history. In spite of the ridicule, the organized campaign of fear, more people have signed this protest against mccarthyism than any notarized petition in human history. They signed in spite of the fact that this admittedly amateurish, underfinanced movement, which tried to recall a senator with less than one-third of the funds normally required to elect one, was never able to reach more than 40 per cent of the state's population with petitions. The miracle isn't that the recall effort fell short of its fabulous goal of 403,000-plus signatures . . . the miracle isn't that so few signed, but that so many signed!

Who are these dastardly, diabolically clever "left-wingers" at which the pro-McCarthy disciples point a finger of frantic warning?

Can they mean Harold Michael, president of the Joe Must Go Club, the heroic marine combat veteran of the Korean War and of World War II, currently chairman of the Polk County Republicans, a dry cleaner in the small northwestern Wisconsin town of Amery?

Can they mean Harry Franke, the conservative Republican state senator from Milwaukee's "silk-stocking" district?

Can they mean able Ivan Nestingen, Democratic attorney from Madison whose services to his city and his state have earned him the respect of leaders in both parties?

Can they mean the two dozen business and professional men, laborers and farmers from widely scattered Wisconsin towns, villages, and cities who comprise the state steering committee, members from both parties who have made all decisions, gathered and expended all funds?

There are veiled hints that they mean me, the first to propose the recall movement, though I have been a Republican for fifty years, including those years in the middle thirties when I witnessed with frowning disapproval the participation of Joseph Raymond McCarthy in what he now chooses to call "Twenty Years of Democratic Treason" as a Democratic candidate and a Democratic worker.

The frenzied attempts to find a jumbo-size halo to fit Joe's expanded cranium and to make a sinister character out of me are good for frequent and unrestrained belly laughs. I recall too well those days not so long ago when Joe, a flamboyant young Irish attorney, joined the staff of conservatively Republican Attorney Mike Eberlein at Shawano. Mike used to come down to the newspaper office at Clintonville, sixteen miles away, shaking his head in confusion. Not only was Joe a Democrat, which was bad enough in Mike's book, but he had a lot of ideas highly embarrassing to his conservative "boss." Joe, already fascinated by headlines, was the first to wear shorts on the staid Shawano golf course.

I recall the week Joseph Raymond left Waupaca to take up the practice of law at nearby Shawano. My old friend, John Burnham, then editor of the Waupaca *Post*, recommended editorially that Joe line his briefcase in pink, and equip himself with a copy of *Das Kapital* and the *Daily Worker*.

Subsequently, Mike's nightmares turned to reality when Joe beat him to the clerk's office with his own nomination papers for the office of circuit judge, an office Mike had coveted during all of his distinguished professional career, and never achieved. Then, as now, friendship was a one-way street on Joe's road map.

But we stray from our subject. We were predicting that a recall effort after November is predestined to success. Under Wisconsin law, qualified signers must be secured in numbers equal to 25 per cent of the total vote for governor in the most recent state election. Those signatures must be secured within sixty days—a thoroughly unfair restraint written into the law when the state's population was considerably smaller than at present. A bill for putting the recall on a fairer basis will be introduced in the next session of the legislature. Democratic Senator Henry Maier of Milwaukee appealed to Governor Kohler during the closing days of the recall campaign to call a special session to revise and liberalize the law, but the governor wasn't hearing well that day.

The November 1954 election will certainly be a much smaller election than the record election of November 1952. The signers of the initial petition, repeating their signatures, will be more than sufficient to recall the junior senator.

The recall committee is cognizant of the errors in the initial campaign. Next time petitions will be in the hands of circulators before the opening gun is fired. Sufficient funds, we hope, will be available at the outset. The bulk of the signatures can be repeated by mail. Unless a minor miracle should occur and the junior senator's stock should suddenly rise in value, a half million signatures can be gathered in three weeks with adequate organization and adequate funds.

The recall committee couldn't duck another effort if the members wanted to duck it. Letters demanding another recall, many of them with small contributions, are still being delivered in Sauk City weeks after the end of the initial recall.

How constitutional is the recall?

It is, of course, thoroughly legal under Wisconsin law. The framers of the Constitution of the United States were undeniably men exceedingly conscious of their individual rights. They did not, unfortunately, contemplate a recall election. But if the courts should hold that the framers of the Constitution contemplated that the United States Senate, which did *not* elect a senator, could impeach him, but the people of his state, who *did* elect him, could not recall him, that decision would be the most ridiculous in American history.

If the pro-McCarthy forces should choose to tie the recall up in the courts, that would not be a wholly undesirable consummation. After all, a McCarthy forced to seek refuge in the courts to protect himself from a suddenly enlightened electorate would have a difficult time playing his favorite role as the Savior of Mankind.

Would the Senate unseat McCarthy, and seat his successor?

The Senate has looked silly enough in its frenzied efforts to make McCarthy look reasonably respectable. They have closed their eyes conveniently to his fantastic financial adventures, his flagrant violations of good taste, his abuse of the truth, his brutal character assassinations. The Senate, we suspect, would welcome an excuse to drop an exceedingly hot potato.

If the Senate refused, the Senate would look pretty silly, but not nearly so silly as a discredited Senator McCarthy. It would be exceedingly interesting to have three senators from Wisconsin in the Senate chambers. Mccarthyism, under those circumstances, would become a national horse laugh.

Since McCarthy would be a candidate in the recall election, could he win by packing the ballot?

The answer is "no." Although that was not its intent, the recall effort has resulted in the most accurate political poll and the most effective political organization in Wisconsin history. If McCarthy were running today he would lose at least 3 to 2, perhaps 2 to 1. While the recall numbers among its leadership no one with senatorial aspirations, and the movement has no ambitions to choose a candidate, the movement is prepared to make such a choice if the situation demands that remedy.

The immediate primary objects of the recall movement are these:

1. A million—two or three million would be better—signatures from other states, subscribing to the recall, as a national demonstration to the Senate that their duty is clear—that the Senate has a clear mandate from the people to unseat Senator McCarthy if the people of Wisconsin elect a successor;

2. A successful recall petition effort followed by a successful recall election early in 1955.

If you are an apostle of mccarthyism, reach for your hat and coat. The show's about over. The People are ready to ring down the curtain.

SOME HAVE

GREATNESS THRUST

UPON THEM...

There are many ways to achieve fame:
 You may publicly swallow live goldfish.
 You may sit on the world's highest flagpole.
 You may drink more beer at a sitting than any living
man.
 You may sleep on a pillow of rattlesnakes.
 You may roll a peanut with your nose from New York
to Los Angeles.
 I chose to start a recall movement against Senator
Joseph McCarthy.
 If I were forced to leave my comfortable obscurity

again, I'm quite sure I would choose one of those simpler routes to the headlines and the air waves.

Amazing things happen to those who seek the recall of Senator McCarthy—things which wouldn't happen if they sought the recall of any other senator, even the President of the United States. I know. These things have happened to me because I launched a movement in Wisconsin as legal as the election process itself.

Merely because I opposed one candidate on what I believed to be moral grounds, I have been read out of the party I have faithfully served without expectation of reward for thirty years by the self-confessed Republican dynasty whose Republicanism has mostly been less loyal and of shorter duration than mine. I have been threatened with eviction from my home town by a half dozen neighbors and businessmen with a grotesque conception of democracy. My life has been threatened, my family has been threatened, my property has been threatened by hundreds of anonymous letters and telephone calls. Never since the days of the Ku Klux Klan have I seen anything like this. Never, I hope, will I see anything like this again.

On the other hand, I have seen myself pictured as a gallant knight in shining armor, a role for which I am wholly unfitted by natural endowment of body and soul. Circumstances have compelled me to become an orator, a television and radio performer, when I have no stomach or gift for any of them.

For thirty years I have been a thoroughly respectable, thoroughly conservative, thoroughly Republican country editor. On Thursday of each week, for 1,560 consecutive weeks, I have taken a firm and uncompromising stand against such obvious evils as sin, the Democratic party, and, all too recently, those who regarded Senator McCarthy as something less than a Grade-A saint.

Several months ago, however, my conscience began to trouble me. If the difficulty had been with my prostate at my not-too-tender age, I would have understood and accepted the situation with proper resignation. But my conscience hasn't bothered me since that eventful day back in the fourth grade when I slipped a garter snake in the teacher's desk during the noon hour. For many years I have had my conscience firmly under control, and my recent symptoms puzzled me no end.

Ultimately, I diagnosed my affliction as an acute and chronic attack of ingrown mccarthyism, a most severe ailment against which even the wonder drugs of this wonder age are powerless.

Just when I began to turn against McCarthy I am not prepared to say. During the 1952 election I supported the junior senator with considerable vigor, even though I had no illusions about his personal and political honesty, or his phony talents as a Communist hunter. In Washington, D. C., any taxi driver can tell you that the senator's Communist hunting technique is about as effective as burning the house down to get rid of a few cockroaches in the kitchen sink.

During my fifty undistinguished years I had presumed myself to be a good citizen and a good Christian. I had attended worship regularly, I had diligently tithed, I had taught Sunday school, I had successfully avoided the toils

of the law, I had mostly voted a straight Republican ticket.
These virtues, I had assumed, would make quite an impression on St. Peter come Judgment Day.

I found nothing inconsistent about my support of Senator McCarthy on the one hand and my smug virtue on the
other. The junior senator was endorsed by the Republican
party. I was a good Republican. It was that simple. I found
the McCarthy medicine a little bitter at times, but like the
child making a wry face as he obediently swallows his
castor oil, I took refuge in the conviction that the bitter
medicine was good for me, and good for my country. My
party said so. Render unto Caesar what is Caesar's. Those
stirring sermons delivered by my pastor were fine for Sun-
day-morning sanctity, but the rest of the week a man had
to be practical.

I am not certain precisely what reasons were most important in prompting me to divorce myself from mccarthyism, and the reasons aren't too important anyway.
Practically everybody has his own reasons for deserting
mccarthyism. They're all good reasons, and several million
people seem to have been smitten with some or most of
them simultaneously.

I can, however, recall the exact moment of my conver-
sion to anti-mccarthyism. One night I sat watching television at the home of a friend whose twelve-year-old
daughter has long been a favorite of mine. Senator McCarthy was attacking one of his political foes with his customary political irresponsibility. The identity of the foe
makes little difference. It was McCarthy's famed Twenty
Years of Treason speech which he has directed succes-

sively against Acheson, Truman, Stevenson, and many others. The script is always the same, except for a substitution of new names to suit his slanderous purposes.

"Is Mr. Truman *really* a traitor?" the little girl wanted to know.

"Of course not," I assured her.

"Why does Senator McCarthy say he's a traitor?" she persisted.

"Politics," I explained learnedly. "Just politics."

I was ready to quit the discussion, but the girl wasn't. "What's politics?"

"Politics," I floundered, "is the method we use to run our government."

The little girl looked horrified. "You mean we run our government with lies?"

I choked on my well-advertised beer. I was in a corner and I knew it. "O.K., Jackie," I said. "You win. Hereafter we won't defend our democracy with lies if I have anything to say about it."

What I was going to do about it I hadn't the faintest idea. Before I went to bed that night I did write an editorial—a sort of open letter to Senator McCarthy recommending that he voluntarily resign from the Senate and take up a career of television wrestling. This still impresses me as a sound, constructive suggestion. Joe, playfully twisting his foe's cauliflower ear when the referee isn't looking, and wailing, "I wuz robbed" in his now historically famous "Point of Order" voice when his shoulders are pinned to the mat, would indubitably be a Grade-A riot among the grunt-and-groan fans.

Subsequently, I appealed to McCarthy to do something
about the growing dairy crisis, but the senator was too
busily engaged in the pursuit of Communists he never
caught. Thereupon I wrote an editorial in which I recommended that, since the junior senator by self-confession
is the only man in the country smart enough to direct the
chase of the Communists, why didn't he take a couple of
hours off some afternoon and sell the 280,000,000-pound
butter surplus?

The results were mildly spectacular, but hardly encouraging. Both editorials got a wide circulation, and in return
I received an avalanche of first-class, second-rate mail.
Mostly, the readers were amused. Quite a few recommended that I book passage to the Russian salt mines, a
trip for which I had no particular enthusiasm since my
family came to this country one hundred eighty-five years
ago and we're beginning to like it here.

Neither suggestion was taken seriously by McCarthy's
office, which has on numerous occasions given considera-
tion to ideas much daffier than these.

Meanwhile, the ghosts of McCarthy's past, present, and
future continued to haunt me.

It was a long and shabby parade.

. . . The desertion of one political party for another in
the interest of political expediency.

. . . Judicial conduct so bad that it brought this well-
earned rebuke from the State Board of Bar Commissioners: "It is difficult to conceive of any conduct which would
bring judges into greater disrepute and contempt than the
conduct of the defendant (McCarthy)."

. . . Shady and slippery financial dealings with such a bad odor that the senator has used all his agile forces to keep them from a public hearing.

. . . The resignation from the United States Marines in one of the most critical moments of the war to run for the United States Senate against young Bob LaFollette.

. . . The shameless exploitation of a phony war record in that campaign.

. . . The open acceptance of support from the then Communist-dominated Wisconsin CIO, and the public praise for Stalin (a few years later this same McCarthy was to ruin the reputations of many a citizen who incurred his displeasure on far more flimsy evidence).

. . . The sad Senate voting record which won for McCarthy the dubious and undisputed title from the working press in Washington as "America's Worst Senator."

. . . The half-truths and the untruths which prompted one news commentator to say: "Senator McCarthy is the one man in public life whom you may safely call a liar without fear of a slander suit."

. . . The character smears on flimsy and fraudulent charges to get a headline or win a convert.

I fought a brief but losing battle with my conscience. It went like this:

ME: Sure, mccarthyism is bad, but maybe evil can be fought only with evil.

CONSCIENCE: Nuts. Never in the history of mankind has a good thing been successfully defended with a bad thing.

ME: But he does fight Communism.

CONSCIENCE: Does he? Let's kick around the notion that

he is a Communist. He'd pretend to chase Commies, but he'd never catch any. He'd clog the newspapers, the airwaves, the United States Senate with drivel so we'd get nothing really constructive done. He'd turn Republicans against Democrats, Republicans against Republicans, Democrats against Democrats, Protestants against Catholics, Catholics against Protestants, neighbor against neighbor. He'd confuse the public thinking. He'd destroy faith in the schools and universities, the churches, the departments of government, the President, the Army, the men behind the H-bomb. What has McCarthy missed on this list? He's attacked everything and everybody short of God.

ME: O.K. . . . O.K. . . . Simmer down. Americans have a sense of humor. They'll laugh him out of office.

CONSCIENCE: I heard that in Berlin back in the early thirties. The Germans were laughing Hitler out of the history books. "That stupid Austrian paperhanger," they chuckled. Six months later he stood them up against a wall and had them shot very, very dead. Give the mccarthyism radicals a good excuse, a sudden, painful twist in history, and they'll shoot *you* very dead.

ME: Listen, bud, I'm fifty years old, and I'm tired. I wanna play around with this country newspaper, take things easy. I gotta mortgage, I wanna play golf and bridge and maybe fish a little. I've worked hard for thirty years to assemble what little worldly goods I possess. Gwan away and quit bothering me. Plenty of guys smarter and richer than I am can fight McCarthy. Me, I've earned a rest.

CONSCIENCE: The smart rich guys won't do it, and you know they won't. They're too busy getting smarter and richer. This is a job for a peanut like you. The history books will never record that you might have licked mccarthyism if you hadn't been so lazy and gutless. But I'll know, and you'll know, and St. Peter will know. If you want to be haunted through the here and the hereafter, you gotta deal, pal.

ME: Look, this thing is too risky. How's one peanut editor gonna persuade 403,000 people to sign a petition? Maybe the whole thing is unconstitutional. Maybe if it is constitutional Joe will pack the ballot and win again anyhow. Maybe the Senate won't unseat Joe, even if the recall works.

CONSCIENCE: You afraid of failure? Son, you're an expert at failure. Anyway, this failure won't be on your conscience. You can live with failure. You've lived with failure many times. But you can't live with a guilty conscience. Write that editorial now. I'm telling you.

ME: You win, but I hate you for it.

Past midnight I sat down at my limping typewriter on that night of March 15, 1954, and hammered out these words:

"There isn't much point in prolonging the suspense of the agony. To be brutally frank, four long years are too many years to wait for an opportunity to shake off the soiled and suffocating cloak of mccarthyism.

"*The Star proposes a recall election in which the sole issue shall be the fitness of Joseph McCarthy to serve his nation, his party, and the sovereign state of Wisconsin.*

"Our decision to call upon the voters of Wisconsin to repudiate the hysterical McCarthy leadership is no whim of the moment. We have pondered, even prayed over it for long, dismal weeks as the genial Irishman we once greatly admired has showered increasing humiliation upon the party and the state to which we have been long devoted.

"IF the people of Wisconsin and the Republican party had been warned a year ago last November that Senator McCarthy was about to use his evil genius for blackmail to undermine the leadership of Dwight D. Eisenhower, the very man upon whose coattails he rode into office . . .

"IF the people and the party had been warned that McCarthy would not only slander one of Wisconsin's most valorous soldiers, but that the senator would toss patriotic caution to the winds, and cast an unfair shadow of incompetence and corruption upon the United Staets Army at a most critical moment in our history when respect and confidence in our armed forces are essential to our national existence . . .

"IF the people and the party had been warned that a dairy crisis would rear its ugly head while the junior senator from America's greatest dairy state would remain silent as a rabbit with laryngitis . . .

"IF the people and party had known all this and much, much more, then we would agree with the handful of gloating Democrats who put party above country as they chuckle: 'We'll do nothing to check McCarthy. Let him put the Republican party out of business.' This selfish, garbled thinking ignores the fairly obvious fact that McCarthy may also put the country out of business.

"In November 1952 the people and the party did *not* know that Senator McCarthy would sabotage the Eisenhower administration in his unscrupulous lust for headlines. In November 1952 McCarthy professed an almost fawning devotion to the Eisenhower leadership. The McCarthy desertion of the Eisenhower leadership is not a story of our manufacture. No less authority than Republican Senator Flanders of Vermont, Vice-President Nixon, and President Eisenhower himself as recently as last week pointed fingers of disillusioned concern at Senator McCarthy.

"The Senator Joseph McCarthy of March 1954 is *not* the man the people of Wisconsin elected to the United States Senate in November 1952.

"Wisconsin need not wait four long years to find out if this has been a tragic case of mistaken identity. Wisconsin can find out *now*. There is a legal, practical procedure for dealing with elected officials who double-cross the people they represent. A recall election is not only possible—it's a moral necessity when the faith of the people has been brazenly violated.

"We are aware of the difficulties which a recall effort must face. The law provides that recall must be requested by signers representing 25 per cent of the gubernatorial vote at the last election. Approximately 1,700,000 votes were cast for governor in that election.

"Undeniably 403,000 names are a lot of names. It is, perhaps, more than a little ludicrous for a small and struggling rural newspaper to play the role of a giant killer. It would be ludicrous except for our confident faith in the hundreds of rural and metropolitan newspapers of the state.

"Wisconsin newspaper editors have all the unfortunate symptoms of the rest of the race, plus a few unique symp-

toms of their own. We quarrel over trivialities. We spout off
at considerable length about great moral truths, and ignore
abuses under our own noses. We call each other 'The One
Party Press,' 'Areacrats,' and a variety of uncomplimentary
names. We profess to believe that our party wears an eternal
halo; we find nothing good in the press and the people whose
faith is in the competing political philosophy.

"But when the odor of iniquity unmistakably assails our
nostrils, the press and the people of Wisconsin have never
failed to rise to the occasion. During the past few weeks we
have talked with hundreds of Wisconsin newsmen of both
political persuasions. They are sick of Senator McCarthy's
blindness and deafness to his people. Even in the face of
this evidence we were not content.

"We asked ourself who might rightfully be offended by
our decision, and we found these answers:

"Certainly not the Republican party. Senator McCarthy,
not those of us who oppose him, has betrayed the party
leadership. McCarthy, unrebuked, may soon officiate at the
funeral rites for Republicanism.

"Certainly not the Catholic Church, which we exceedingly respect even though we are not a member and Joe is.
The faculty members of a great Catholic university and the
editorial direction of a great and influential Catholic publication have vigorously condemned him.

"Certainly not the American Legion, or those who fought
valiantly for their country. In language stronger than ours
the Stoughton veterans of two wars a few days ago exposed
the alarming tactics of McCarthy in his persecution of
General Zwicker, one of Wisconsin's immortal heroes.

"We are aware, however, of certain dire consequences of
our presumption. We shall lose a number of subscribers among

those who profess to read only what they believe. They will, you may be sure, continue to read us, but they wouldn't be caught dead on our subscription list.

"We have been a Republican for more than thirty years, but there are those in the party who will vigorously reject us from the ranks. This will hurt a little, but it will not dissuade us. We have said it before, and we say it again: Wherever a cancer is found, even if it be in our political party, the way to cure it isn't to ignore it, but to cut it out.

"We have long since forfeited the friendship of Joe McCarthy, and we can't afford to lose many friends. We have never ceased to admire and envy the intellectual brilliance, the misdirected courage of the junior senator. Sharply rebuked by his people, Joe McCarthy can still perform great and lasting services for his state, his party, and his nation. Left to his own bizarre devices, Joe McCarthy can only go down in history as a brutal buffoon.

"We should prefer to remain silent on the McCarthy issue. Silence is easy on the blood pressure, and our blood pressure isn't what it once was. But we prefer to live with a higher blood pressure than with an aching, ulcerous conscience. Failure, rebuke, and ridicule have long since ceased to terrify us. We have outlived all of them many times.

"We cannot believe that the newspapers and the people of Wisconsin will shirk an obvious, even if painful, responsibility. Even if they do, we shall never be sorry we made the effort."

I'm no great shakes as a praying man, but I prayed over this one not once but many times. I won't go so far as to say the Lord came out definitely on my side. The pro-McCarthy forces seem to have a copyright on the Lord's support. But I will say that the persistent ulcer on my conscience healed with miraculous rapidity. That night I slept as I hadn't slept for many nights.

Next morning I had a late breakfast. Between sips of coffee I read the editorial to my wife. I studied her face, but after thirty years I still can't predict what's going on in her mind.

"Here goes the new car to replace our 1949 prehistoric Pontiac," she sighed. "Here goes our television set. Here goes our new home, maybe our newspaper. Here goes our quiet, peaceful life."

I made a mock motion to tear the manuscript. "It doesn't have to run."

She put her hand on mine, and shook her head. "Remember back in our college days when you used to look up to Senator George Norris, Norman Thomas, and fighting Bob LaFollette? You didn't have to agree with them. But you used to say: 'The country is safe when its heroes are honest men.' Remember?"

I nodded, not quite understanding.

"What kind of heroes do Gary and his friends talk about? (Gary is our youngest son, just graduated from Stout Institute.) Senator McCarthy who got rich and famous by lies and smears. Even the young divinity students don't talk about the souls they can save. They talk about how they can get the biggest salaries and the biggest congregations. One Joe McCarthy is bad enough. I don't want a generation of them."

I frowned, but I was coming closer to understanding. She squeezed my hand.

"It isn't for us to choose. If we can do one tiny thing to restore the honest example of the Norrises, the Thomases, and the LaFollettes in our country, it's worth what it will cost."

A few weeks later I was to hear almost these same words from the lips of the Milwaukee Mothers March on McCarthy. Women, invariably, think in simpler terms than their men. The mother's instinct to protect her young goes further than physical protection. Instinctively, the mother would shield them from the hazards of the mind and soul as well as the hazards of the body.

The *Star* office is two short blocks from our home. Ten minutes later I hung the editorial on the copy hook. My hand trembled a little. It would have trembled even more if I had known how prophetic my words really were.

From my office desk I saw Butler Delaney, shop foreman who was setting type that morning, pull the editorial from the hook. I saw him fold the copy, place it in the rack, and his agile fingers—among the fastest in Wisconsin—began to dance over the keyboard of the mad machine that Mergenthaler built. Suddenly he rared back in his chair, whistled, and called to the crew:

"Cripes! All hell's gonna break loose in Wisconsin, and we're right in the middle of it!"

I'm not sure what I anticipated as we put the paper to bed that Wednesday night of March 18. In any event, what I anticipated had little in common with what happened.

Our little newspaper office was reasonably calm Thursday morning, but this was the last hour of serenity we were to enjoy for many weeks to come. When I returned from lunch I found five notes on my desk:

"Call New York, operator." . . . "Call Detroit, operator." . . . "Call Los Angeles, operator." . . . "Call St. Louis, operator." . . . "Call Minneapolis, operator."

Then, and not until then, did I know that I had a lion by the tail.

THE SPREADING

GRASS ROOTS...

If there's any doubt in your mind that this was a bungling, amateurish movement with its origins in the heart rather than the head, this should dispel it: the news of the recall had spread all around the globe before a single petition was available.

One of the intriguing charges made against me by the pro-McCarthy crowd was the whimsical suggestion that I'd launched a recall movement to stimulate business for the *Star's* printing department. The fact is that the *Star* isn't in the printing business. We confine our activities to publishing a newspaper. We did print the first few thousand petitions on a small hand press because commercial

printers couldn't serve us fast enough, but we couldn't and
didn't profit one nickel by the Joe Must Go movement.

The first petition was still a little damp, fresh from the
press, as I carefully carried it downtown to the morning
"coffee conference." These 10 A.M. "bull sessions" are fairly common in Wisconsin small towns. Business and professional men, farmers and laborers flock in like steel fil-
ings speeding to a magnet. In thirty minutes of coffee
and conversation the sick world is miraculously cured on
a local, state, national, and international level, but the
cure is only a temporary one. Next morning the world is
just as sick as ever.

Sauk-Prairie invariably confounds the experts who look
for devious reasons in explaining the pro-McCarthy phe-
nomena. Sauk City is largely Roman Catholic, yet Sauk
is one of the few rural communities that slapped Joe down
—by one vote—in the 1952 election, in spite of my advice
to the contrary. Prairie is largely Protestant, and in 1952
was largely pro-McCarthy. Yet more Prairie citizens signed
petitions, even though they didn't make so much noise
about it. Mostly, they'd call my home at night, and ask
that I bring a petition over. They'd make it perfectly clear
that they didn't want their neighbors to know. Sometimes
they'd mention the very neighbors who had signed a petition an hour before with an identical request.

The druggist was behind the counter, and three local
citizens sat on high stools. You can guess the subject of
their conversation. I laid the petition down in front of
them. August Derleth reached for it. "Augie" is our local
celebrity. He's written a hundred successful books and un-

counted hundreds of shorter stories. Politically, he's an Independent. It was something of a historic moment—the first of what I hoped, without much optimism, would ultimately be 403,000-plus signatures.

I wasn't at all surprised when Dr. Bachhuber, a stanch Democrat, signed. But the druggist's signature was something of a surprise. He was Sauk's most active Republican. During the 1952 campaign a huge painting of Eisenhower had adorned the side of his building. He signed with no more hesitation than the others.

A little red-faced, he turned to the Democrat:

"I've had enough."

I went back to the *Star* office feeling something like David might have felt just after Goliath made that historic three-point landing on his schnozzle, tummy, and toes.

Bedlam is a modest word for the *Star* premises. The morning mail had come in. We hadn't suspected there was this much mail in all of Wisconsin. Both phones were ringing, and the local depot agent hurried in with a fistful of telegrams.

"It's great," said my foreman, "but it's a helluva place to put out a newspaper."

In the midst of the frenzied voices on the telephone came one that was calm and firm. "My name is Harold Michael. I'm Polk County Republican chairman. I've just been reading your recall editorial at Palmer Sondreal's Amery *Free Press* office. I was a marine in World War II. I'm a marine combat veteran of the Korean War. If you can use a conservative Republican who feels his political and moral responsibilities very keenly at this moment, I'm with you all the way."

Saturday's mail was even heavier. The *Star's* staff of five worked long into the night to keep up with it. Volunteers flocked in to help—Democrats and long-time McCarthy foes—recently disillusioned Republicans—mothers of no political faith who just didn't like "what this man is doing to the morality of our children."

Our 4,000 petitions had shrunk to 500. They were gone early in the evening. But a nearby printer had promised 10,000 more Monday morning.

Monday the *Star* received more mail than the rest of the postal patrons in the village. Press photographers were there to record it. So were two television cameras. It was quite a day.

Tex McCrary called from New York to take a telephone transcription for his newscast.

The Associated Press called for a comment on McCarthy's statement that he'd never heard of me. I suddenly found the company much better among those Joe had forgotten than among those he remembered.

Out of the confusion came the "Joe Must Go" slogan, and the campaign trademark—Joe riding through a forest of Texas oil wells and cactus in a Cadillac.

The telephone wouldn't stop ringing. At 2 A.M. two inebriated gentlemen, who identified themselves as O'Reilly and O'Rourke, called from St. Paul. The conversation, accompanied by background noises which indicated O'Reilly and O'Rourke were inhabiting premises hardly recommended for good Irishmen, went like this:

O'REILLY: Why have you started this despicable anti-Catholic movement?

ME: I have started a movement to recall Senator McCarthy, but it isn't an anti-Catholic movement. In fact, three members of your faith were working with me tonight.

O'ROURKE: The Pope will excommunicate 'em.

ME: I doubt it. One is chairman of the fund-raising committee.

O'ROURKE: The Pope will excommunicate him as soon as he gets the money raised.

I made a commendable effort to persuade O'Reilly and O'Rourke that this wasn't a religious issue, and that I continued to live in peace among my Catholic neighbors, but I had a discouraged feeling that somehow I had failed.

Each morning, for two weeks, at a quarter to six, a lady with a quavering voice called from a nearby country line to ask the same question: "Why don't you give all this money to the church instead of fighting this good man?"

The telephone calls, the letters, the telegrams and the post cards continued to average 75 to 1 anti-McCarthy. One of the most welcome telephone calls came from Ed Sachs, a capable newsman who had recently resigned from the Milwaukee *Sentinel* to write a novel.

Sympathetic of the plight that faced me, Ed offered to postpone his novel so that he might edit my newspaper until the end of the campaign. It was the best news I'd heard since the night the schoolhouse caught fire when I was in the fifth grade.

Mr. Sachs' prediction about our newspaper problems was a masterly piece of understatement. Letters spilled

over from our small office into the shop. Mr. Butler Delaney, our customarily non-complaining shop foreman,
complained in aggrieved tones:

"I been looking for four hours for Kundert's ad. I just
found it in the middle of the vicious, malicious, and threatening pro-McCarthy file. The type faces are so corroded
I got to reset the ad."

Mr. Cecil Ragatz, the exceedingly pleasant and efficient
gentleman of Swiss ancestry who runs our office, was even
more unhappy.

"I keep telling myself," he said, "that my desk must be
under that pile of McCarthy mail, but I haven't seen it in
so long I'm beginning to be tortured by doubts."

It was apparent even to a peanut country editor that the
recall movement had outgrown us. I called for help in a
loud voice. Specifically, I called a state recall meeting at
Riverview Ballroom, largest gathering place available in
Sauk City, for the following Sunday.

Not since I paced the hospital corridor at Lincoln, Nebraska, twenty-four years ago awaiting the birth of our
first son had I experienced a sensation quite like the one
I experienced that Sunday. The hall was an elegant sight,
thanks chiefly to Jack Voll, a Madison sales promoter who
lives in Sauk City and wields a magic paintbrush.

But the weather was miserable. A sharp wind from
northern Wisconsin and maybe the North Pole was spit-
ting a steady and discouraging barrage of fluffy snow-
flakes. I was smitten with a tardy and awesome fear that
I'd feel pretty silly if only a double handful of people appeared. I was pretty sure my wife, the loyal members of

my newspaper staff, and a couple of intimate friends would be on hand. Outside of that I had no very clear notion of what was about to happen.

The presence of two TV cameras, a movie film service, and a dozen reporters and cameramen from metropolitan newspapers added little to my peace of mind. The event had been hastily and poorly publicized. I found myself trying to choose between eloquent excuses for the lack of an audience or departing hastily for Mexico City.

The meeting was scheduled for 3 P.M. At two-thirty the big hall was almost deserted. I was summoned to the newspaper office to pose for TV "movies," later used on Eric Severeid's American Week show. When I returned to the hall twenty minutes later, I had to elbow my way into the hall. Inside, there wasn't even standing room. Sally and Gene, who run the place, estimated the crowd inside at 800, and the boys outside estimated that an equal number had been turned away.

I felt considerably better.

At three-five Ivan Nestingen, the tall, Norwegian attorney from Madison who was to serve as meeting chairman, tapped me on the shoulder. "Let's get this show on the road."

If the preacher says as nice things about me at my funeral as Ivan did in his introduction that afternoon, Saint Peter should be mightily impressed. I managed to get up by laboriously straightening my knees, which had suddenly turned to rubber in the remarkable alchemy of fear. I hadn't made a speech since I spoke out boldly for Philippine independence on the Aububon, Iowa, high-school debate team back in 1922.

I was thankful for the blinding floodlamps in front of me which mercifully blotted out the audience. The cheers and the applause were deafening. For a moment I reflected: "You're a big wheel. These cheers are for you." But my conscience told me something different. The cheers weren't for me. The cheers were only an expression of a dim, desperate hope—a hope that Wisconsin might not have to endure four more long years of mccarthyism.

I reflected on the copies of the rural newspapers that had reached my desk during the three preceding days. Most of them were with us. The handful against us took a peculiar position. None of them had anything to say about McCarthy or mccarthyism. They had plenty to say about me. I was a brazen headline hunter. I was seeking publicity to increase the value of my newspaper property. I hadn't yet learned that denial only adds fuel to the fires of those whose only answer to an issue is the accusation of phony motives in those who disagree with them. I attempted to defend myself, which was probably a waste of time, since those who believed in me required no defense, and those who didn't believe in me wouldn't listen anyway. This is what I said:

"I anticipated that the friends of Senator McCarthy would accuse me of being a headline hunter, and their accusations have considerably exceeded my expectations. But I want to assure you that I have been too long engaged in the cynical trade of reporting the foibles and triumphs of the human race to fall for the fallacy that I have suddenly achieved greatness. For fifty years I have been a very small frog in very small puddles. The moment this recall issue is resolved one way or another I shall be the same small frog in the same small puddle . . . .

"Already the recall campaign has had one healthy effect. For months Senator McCarthy has enjoyed a virtual political monopoly on the air waves, the TV screens, the newspaper and magazine pages. Whatever our opinions of the man may be, he is undeniably news. The recall movement has given the press, the radio, and television an opportunity to toss frequent and fairly effective rebuttal at him. It has given them a chance to show the world that many, many thousands of Wisconsin electors sought only a rallying point at which to demonstrate their disapproval."

There was plenty of amateur oratory that afternoon. Heads and hands popped up all over the hall, their owners seeking a chance to speak at the "mike." It was like an old-fashioned southern camp meeting. A father of two ex-servicemen said mccarthyism threatened to destroy the values for which his sons had fought. An elderly woman came to the stage to tell me that she had just changed her mind about mccarthyism, and "I feel like I've just taken a bath."

There had been threats of physical violence from the pro-McCarthy faction. These threats had worried Sally and Gene, who own the ballroom. While we doubted the necessity for it, we had requested the presence of village and county police officers. The bluecoats were there, strategically and conspicuously placed around the hall and in the corridors.

There was no violence, but two pro-McCarthy spectators did shout their way into the program. At one point a leather-lunged young man screamed: "Why is it that more people in Wisconsin are against McCarthy than are against Communism?"

I tried to be calm about it. "I don't believe it's true. In any event, I refuse to have my Americanism tested by one man. That's the test Adolf Hitler imposed upon his people. That's the test every dictator in the history of mankind has imposed upon his people."

A local restaurant proprietor, who waves the flag with great diligence, identified himself as a "one-hundred-percent pure American." He wanted to know if there were any significance "to the American flag being on the left of the speaker rather than on his right where it belongs!"

Jack Bauer, a National Guard lieutenant in charge of hall arrangements, offered to answer the question.

"If the flag is on the stage with the speaker," he explained patiently, "it must be to the speaker's right. If the flag is on the floor with the audience, as this flag is, it must be on the right of the audience."

The heckler disappeared. Fifteen minutes later he approached me, waving what he said was a flag manual, and demanding time at the microphone to read from it. Unfortunately, the chairman had adjourned the meeting, the audience was filing out, and it would have been an impossible task to re-assemble them. This was doubtless a great pity, and the repercussions were noisy and numerous. I hadn't heard the last of this local heckler, whose frustrated "100-per-cent pure Americanism" led him to extravagances which considerably exceeded the ambitious imaginative efforts of Lewis Carroll, Aesop, and Hans Christian Andersen.

The organization meeting of the state Joe Must Go steering committee was a revelation in what had happened to the popularity of the junior senator in Wisconsin. The committee speedily elected Harold Michael, the young, handsome Amery dry cleaner as chairman of the Joe Must Go movement. He was a good choice, for he was politically "untouchable" and no one could find a single hole in his armor of political virtue. There were other surprises in the committee membership. Disillusionment was an epidemic among those who had followed the junior senator too long and too far.

But the most amazing and cheering "convert" was Carl Lachmund of Sauk City. Carl, a lifelong conservative Republican whose family helped to found Sauk City, is a lumberman in the village. I personally requested that he serve as treasurer of the group, even though I wasn't quite certain of the strength of his convictions when I made the request. Carl was summoned to the meeting by telephone, and informed of the request. The struggle with his conscience was obvious on his honest, open features. He cleared his throat.

"I am aware of the consequences," he said slowly. "I know full well that I will lose friends and customers. But it's time for us Americans to stand up and be counted on this issue. I accept."

I was very proud of Carl Lachmund at that moment.

QUACK! QUACK!...

The letters and press comments and a modest stream of small money from the "little people" kept pouring in. The Joe Must Go headquarters were moved to the basement of Riverview Hotel. Cecil Ragatz found his desk, and Butler Delaney no longer had to dig advertisements out of a mountain of vicious and threatening pro-McCarthy letters. Ed Sachs arrived and I turned the reins of the newspaper over to him with a sigh so heavy it could be heard as far south as Madison.

Sachs could double for Ichabod Crane without stretching an inch or losing a pound. He constantly wears on his thin features the caustic expression of a man whose wife has just run away with his chauffeur and his favorite fly-casting rod. Since Ed has never been married, has no ambitions in that direction, and hates fishing, this "I-dare-you-to-make-me-smile" expression is doubtless the sad result of associating with city editors for ten years. It is this expression that causes girls at the newsstands in hotel lobbies to chirp, "That will be five cents, please," the minute Sachs picks up an evening paper and before he has a chance to reach into his pocket. For four cents they trust him, but not for a nickel.

With my vast background of judging newspaper characters, I immediately identified Sachs' expression as a phony mask concealing a chromium-plated soul. One little thing bothered me considerably: he shamelessly admitted he couldn't drive an automobile. I've met a couple of guys who neither know nor care where the Milwaukee Braves stand in the National League, and I've learned to accept them with the rest of the human race, but a guy thirty years old who couldn't drive an automobile in this year of our Lord 1954 was certainly suspect. Sachs, I discovered, had a theory about driving automobiles.

"So long as I don't learn to drive," he philosophized, "I'm technically a pedestrian. Pedestrians are only mad at automobile drivers. The minute I learn to drive, I begin to lead a double life. When I'm behind a wheel, I'm mad at pedestrians; when I'm walking, I'm mad at motorists. I just don't want to be mad at everybody."

Sachs, having been reared exclusively on a skim-milk metropolitan newspaper diet, had a little trouble showing proper enthusiasm for those creamy small-town news sensations like the Ladies' Aid having pot luck with Mrs. Zwiebach, but he had a better time in the news columns than he had anticipated, and so did the readers.

Up in Hayward, where Republicans are thicker than muskies, my friend Editor Julian Gingrass, one of Joe's twelve apostles in Wisconsin, recommended that the state press association "investigate Gore." Carl Zielke, executive secretary of the Wisconsin Press Association, suffered a sudden and acute attack from his chronic stomach ulcers, and vigorously voiced his conviction that the WPA would avoid the recall issue like the plague.

Gingrass countered with a proposal to organize a "Communists Must Go" Club. He offered to collect money and forward any balances to Senator McCarthy to fight the Kremlin. It had never occurred to Gingrass, apparently, that anyone other than Joe McCarthy is capable of fighting Communism. To Julian the anti-Communism movement was a one-man crusade, with the simon-pure friends of democracy on one side and the anti-McCarthy reds, pinks, and left-wingers on the other.

There were other sour notes among our exchanges. Ellsworth Coe, the exceedingly witty editor of the Whitewater *Register,* labeled the Joe Must Go movement as a "grass-roots movement—all quack."

Speaking before the 300 members of a new Joe Must Go Club at Superior the following Sunday, Harold Michael reminded Editor Coe that "quack grass is the fastest-growing, fastest-spreading, and hardest to kill of all the grasses."

But Editor Coe would not be denied his last word. Scrapping his sense of humor, he not only accused me of shameless headline hunting, but of launching the recall to enhance the value of my newspaper so I could sell at a fancy price.

This was about as logical as charging George Washington with starting the American Revolution so he could get the British over here and sell them lots in Manhattan.

The Fort Atkinson newspaper, which I edited for a number of years, was singularly and similarly concerned lest my proposal to recall Jumbled Joe should envelop me in a thoroughly undeserved cloak of fame. The Broadhead newspaper concurred in this unflattering interpretation of my motives.

Things were confusing enough at this point even if anti-McCarthy Publisher Witte of the Mauston newspapers and pro-McCarthy Publisher Schwindler of the Mosinee newspaper hadn't become embroiled in a private feud, during which the issue of mccarthyism was hopelessly lost among the debris of journalistic reputations.

Wisconsin rural newspapers are roughly—and I use roughly advisedly—divided into two schools:

1. The larger school which won't even say it's a nice day without taking a poll of the Chamber of Commerce and the city council;
2. The rugged individualists whose shoulders chronically carry enough chips to fuel a University of Wisconsin homecoming bonfire.

The latter group, especially the pro-McCarthy faction, had no apparent concern with the recall issue. It was more

fun to jump upon a fellow editor and kick his teeth down
his throat. In Wisconsin the country editors play the political game unhampered by Marquis of Queensberry rules.
For instance, this was the opening salvo from the sul-
phuric pen of Editor Coe:

GLORY GORE, THE OPPORTUNIST

"I picked the worst week in the year to park in a hospital
at Madison. It was the week Editor Gore chose to prove the
grass roots at Sauk City are quack. But being in an ulcerous
mood, it is not too late to express my personal feelings about
Glory Gore, the opportunist.

"Gore is a headline hunter who has squatted in the short
shadow of the *Capitol Times* for too long.

"Why wait six months, Gore? Did it look as though Mc-
Carthy was licked and this was the logical time for the small
dogs to close in for a bite at the carcass?

"Joe's enemies have accused him of grabbing the Communist issue to get headlines. I see a similarity there, Gore.

"I'm interested in the names of the '200 editors I've talked
to.' Don't count me among them.

"Your inaccuracies are a little revolting. Just which fairway
on the golf course did you let Joe shoot through? Ah, yes, I
know him well.

"You have handed yourself to the enemy on a silver platter.
Even a wee little editor with cataracts on both eyes can see
that everything is being done to split the Republican party
wide open. And you, Gore, have given them the big break.

"I wish you luck on the signatures and a recall election
would suit me just fine!"

Meanwhile some forty rural newspapers had rushed to our defense. Some of them were flatly committed to the view that mccarthyism is a moral issue, and the only way to restore the morality of Wisconsin is to erase mccarthyism. Others merely were of the opinion that there has been a tremendous change in Wisconsin sentiment toward McCarthy, and that the recall effort was the only practical process of demonstrating the change.

A little jarring was the attitude of Wisconsin's two most powerful newspapers—the Milwaukee *Journal* and the Madison *Capital Times*—both long-time foes of McCarthy. Both took a dim view of the recall movement for many weeks. There were too many risks, and they felt that failure might react to McCarthy's advantage.

Most amusing product of the "opposition of friends" was this morbid piece from the facile pen of Miles McMillin, a *Capital Times* editor:

THE WRONG OX MAY BE GORED

"Leroy Gore, the editor and publisher of the Sauk City *Star*, which most assuredly will be known from now on as 'the Sauk City weekly issue of the *Daily Worker*' among the followers of you-know-who, has a good fast ball but his latest pitch runs the grave risk of being knocked out of the park. Instead of keeping it over the outside corner, he has laid it down over the heart of the plate.

"Mr. Gore has launched a campaign to recall Senator McCarthy from the U.S. Senate. While this is the consummation of consummations and a project that will win him unalloyed blessings from all men of good will, it must be noted that the

genial philosopher from Augie Derleth's precincts is juggling
a couple of beakers of political nitro.

"I do not speak of the mayhem that may befall him when
the McCarthy pack turns on him. Mr. Gore, though a com-
paratively young man, is one of those old-fashioned Americans who isn't afraid of a gouging session. Although he's
dead wrong about a number of things, he has a deep and
abiding appreciation of the ancient American right to be
wrong and to advertise it to the world every hour on the hour.
Leroy Gore takes the position that he's got rights that he's
never even used, although any impartial committee would
be hard put to find any that not only has he used but which
he has not exploited unmercifully.

"It is a waste of worry to concern oneself about the fact
that he is out inviting the lightning to strike. He'll take whatever lightning has to offer and return more of the same.

"There has been a sharp burst of interest in the recall question in recent days, and there is no doubt that the interest
is running high. Those who argue that it should be tried seem
to think that there would be little trouble in getting the required signatures. They point out that Tom Fairchild got
more than 400,000 votes in the 1952 campaign against Mc-
Carthy, as indeed he did.

"Getting votes in a secret polling place is one thing. Getting the same people to put their names on a petition in the
present atmosphere of hysteria is quite another.

"Perhaps McCarthy is skidding faster than I think he is.
Leroy Gore may hear some rumblings on the Sauk prairie
that are more audible than they are around Capitol Square.
It might be that 450,000 people would be willing to state
publicly what the United States Senate, with full knowledge
of what has been going on, has been afraid to state.

"But if there isn't, McCarthy is going to be handed a valuable weapon for some psychological blitzkrieging at a time when he needs it rather badly. It seems to me that the trouble with Gore's idea is that the wrong ox may be Gored."

The 8,000 letters received during these first few days presented an interesting pattern. The Wisconsin letters were consistently 75 to 1 anti-McCarthy. The out-of-state letters were consistently 2 to 1 "anti-us." Practically all of the malicious, obscene, and threatening letters were among the out-of-state mail.

A few of our critics were funny. A Kentucky Baptist warned us: "Don't let them take any more pictures of you. You look like a Methodist."

This, I assumed, was the Kentucky Baptist's idea of the pinnacle of insults. Personally, I have no very clear mental picture of what a Methodist is supposed to look like, but if the newspaper and television photos of me are typical of the Methodist countenance, aesthetically the Methodists leave considerable to be desired.

Mr. Butler Delaney, shop foreman—a combat veteran of World War II and a stanch Republican—wrote the *Star* editorial that week:

FEAR

"While reading the thousands of letters received during the past week and filing them in their proper files, I observed that the one thing that stands out in these letters is FEAR within the writers, and the desperate eagerness which has inspired their writing these letters, as though this FEAR had for a long time been building up within themselves, and now that opportunity presents itself they are, like myself, grabbing at the opportunity to voice their opinions. It looks as though all they have been waiting for is for someone to open the doorway for them (as Mr. Gore has done), so that once more an American citizen can openly express his views or be critical of a public official without immediately being condemned as a Communist, Traitor, Subversive, or some other name which has been thrown around so promiscuously of late, and so we can revert to the form of Americanism which we have all fought for since the Revolutionary War and the forming of the Constitution which gave us these rights and privileges.

"The general tone of the overwhelming majority of anti-McCarthy letters which come from clergymen of many denominations—Protestant ministers and Catholic priests, school principals and teachers, professional men, farmers, housewives, and people of all categories is their heartfelt appreciation to Mr. Gore for his opening of a way for them—some FEAR it is already too late—that the McCarthy machine has already grown to the point where Mr. Gore will be smashed by clever political methods, perhaps even driven out of business the same as those who opposed Hitler were smashed when they woke up too late to realize that their right to oppose or criticize was gone. Some plead not to use their name for fear McCarthy will brand them as a Communist for speaking up against him, which may cause them to lose their job and the ability to support their family. Some FEAR with prayers for Mr. Gore's safety and well-being.

"It is regrettable that every man, woman, and child in the nation cannot have the opportunity I have had to read these letters from all parts of the state and nation, to see what people have been keeping within themselves, how they feel, how they have grasped desperately at what many of them feel is a last chance, and maybe even too late to speak up and say what they think and how they have come to FEAR the Mc-Carthy machine to the point where soon, had not this way been opened to them by a small-town newspaperman with courage, they would not have dared to speak at all."

One morning a Mr. Cooper appeared at our office. Mr. Cooper is an investigator for Mr. Fulton Lewis, who conducts a purported newscast over numerous stations of the Mutual Broadcasting Company radio network. I showed Mr. Cooper a file of obscene and threatening letters four inches thick.

"This," I said, "is a bit of required reading preceding an interview."

Mr. Cooper spent a quarter-hour skimming through the file.

"I'm interested," I said, "in knowing how you explain this kind of a following for a man whom you presume does only good. If we were recalling Senator Wiley or even President Eisenhower we would not get this kind of a response. A great many people would protest that we were making a grave mistake, but they would not threaten to murder us, to kidnap our children, to blow up our newspaper, or even to ship us to the Russian salt mines."

Our question is still unanswered.

Unfortunately, most of the pro-McCarthy mail is unprintable. Much of it is criminal, if the identity of the anonymous authors could be established. Of the milder letters we reproduce a few paragraphs to indicate the mentally warped nature of these pro-McCarthy followers. The only deletions have been those necessitated by legal restrictions:

"Skunk Gore: You dirty ——— Red. I know more people who are for McCarthy than you do who are against him. You so & so what the hell of a difference will it make if he wrecks the Democrat and Republican parties—both parties can go to the devil. The American people should wake up and create an American party. Ike is becoming as much a Red Herring as Truman. Above all dont forget that only Reds and Homosexuals attack McCarthy. So I guess you must be either one of them. The reason those Red rats and dirty homosexuals attack McCarthy is because of his exposure of them in our lousy form of government."

"Mr. Gore. I think you are a great editor. No, by Gosh, I think you are the greatest editor in whole wide world and in my opinion you are doing a terrific job. Please excuse crayon because they won't let us have anything sharp in here."

"You Rat! I hope the newspaper association deports you. . . . Judas was a gentleman compared to you. Couldn't that dunce you are married to put you on the right track?"

"Leroy Gore? Drop dead."

"All the Freemasons, all the depraved Socialists, all the Communists, all the adulterous Democrats, all the birth-control advocates, all the hate-mongers, all the thieving atheists . . . all the filthy swine of America congratulate you in your campaign against Senator Joseph McCarthy! If you can raise enough Hell, you may be able to defeat the Senator who has the backing of Heaven itself!"

"You had better take the next boat to Russia, period. I am sure that the Real Americans in Wisconsin will finally get to you and take care of you the way all filthy Communists are finally disposed of in this country. It is really not surprising that you are able to get these Wisconsin people to fall for your crap and communist ideas since the University of Wisconsin was about the first State University that embraced communist."

"I am writing to Senators Mundt, Velde, and President Eisenhower to have you investigated."

"My advice to a dumb-head—2 by 4, hickish country editor is to keep your nose where it belongs or someone will knock it there for you."

. "Stop picking on McCarthy leave him alone because if you don't you will GO SO FAST you won't know what hit you."

On the other hand, we received amazing support from sources which were a little surprising. I quote a few typical samples:

From a Texas publisher: "I do not envy you for the recriminations that are sure to come your way from the senator and his supporters, and yet I admire you for taking a public stand against him. The people of Wisconsin will be doing themselves and the nation at large a great favor if they will recall McCarthy."

From a veteran: "I am a member of the American Legion and very proud of it, but the Legion does not attempt to tell its members how to think, speak, or vote. Consequently, I cannot, or will not, on the other hand, as a member, speak for the Legion as a group. I feel that the work Legionnaires and all other ex-servicemen are doing to help the Joe Must Go movement is strictly a matter of individual citizenship and patriotism and not as a part of any group movement. I sin-

cerely feel that every ex-serviceman in Wisconsin as a citizen
should immediately acquaint himself with the true facts behind mccarthyism and get behind the recall movement while
there is still a chance to eliminate this menacing cloud of
dictatorship which is creeping over our state and nation . . . .
Now is the time for action before it is too late."

From a prominent Catholic clergyman: "Congratulations on
your vision and initiative in starting action for the recall of
Senator McCarthy.

"You have boosted the morale of all those who still believe
in reason and in freedom and in the sacredness of human
beings.

"To your success!"

From a Southern housewife: "You, more than anyone in
Washington, have steadied our nerves here in the South just
a little. You can't know how humiliated we 'turn-coat Democrats' have been to have this crusade turn into something just
as slimy as what we had before. I feared a socialized state
but the actions of Mr. McCarthy and his smart-alec crowd
have really frightened me. Was Hitler's method of gaining
power much different?

"We writhe in indignation at the smug way that they throw
their weight around. When the President of the United States
and the entire Army trembles before such men it really knocks
the props from under all of us.

"We were told that you, in Wisconsin, adored him. We
were told that no one dared cross him.

"Congratulations from the bottom of my heart. All we want
is good government from whichever side is willing to give it
to us.

"What must the world think of us? How can we influence

other countries away from Communism by the example of
men who will do anything to gain power?

"We love you."

"Perhaps you would be interested to know why you received this letter and contribution from the northern part of
Minnesota. I was born in Turkey and I came to the U. S. when
I was 16. I know what it means to live under constant fear that
someone is going to spy on you or accuse you of saying something against the Ottoman empire which compares a great deal
to mccarthyism. McCarthy uses the same tactics in that someone who doesn't agree with him is a pro-Communist or a fellow traveler. He has insulted some of the most intelligent people in the United States because they do not agree with him.

"As I write to you about mccarthyism, I am fully aware of
what would happen to us free-thinking people and believers
in good honest government if McCarthy's faction roots much
deeper. I know for myself I'd rather die than to live under a
government that you fear.

"We have many friends and relatives in Wisconsin and we
have written several letters expressing our feeling toward
Sen. McCarthy and most of them have changed their opinion
from the day that he won the election two years ago.

"Keep up the good work and if you need more money we
will come to your aid."

From a senator of another state: "Please accept my congratulations, best wishes, and a token of material support of your
recall election project.

"You may be contributing as important a factor to life on
this planet as any other of modern times."

The biggest news of the week was the announcement
of Fred Zimmerman, Secretary of State of Wisconsin, who

polled more votes in November 1952 than any politician in Wisconsin history, that he believed in the recall movement. Fred signed a petition and defined mccarthyism:

"Mccarthyism breaks most of the laws of God and man. All McCarthy does is go around making everybody hate everybody else."

"INNOCENTS ABROAD"

Geographically, Wisconsin is a politician's nightmare. Most of the Democrats, most of the industry, and most of the population are concentrated along the eastern border. Westward lies "America's Dairyland," where the population is thinner, the Republicans thicker among the rolling, wooded hills, the valley grasslands, and along the borders of Wisconsin's matchless lakes.

Early in the recall effort we had to make a decision. It was fairly obvious that we might easily gather the required 403,000-plus signatures from the eastern borders of the state by concentrating all of our efforts and our slim funds there.

But an industrially sponsored recall would be as vulnerable as a nudist at a clothing convention. In most Wisconsin elections the dairy farmers hold the balance of power. If McCarthy were to be defeated, we had to carry our campaign into the "cow country."

We weren't gullible enough to even hope that we could completely organize all of Wisconsin in sixty days. The Democratic party has never been able to do that job in western Wisconsin where Democrats are spread out fairly thin.

Wisconsin farmers gave McCarthy his 140,000 margin of victory in 1952, when he was carried into office on Eisenhower's coattails. The President and Governor Walter Kohler won by a third of a million, and Wisconsin's champion vote getter, Secretary of State Fred Zimmerman, won by well over a half million.

At the *Star* we know considerable about farmers. For two consecutive years we have won the American Dairy Association award for "distinguished service to the dairy industry." I was spending two days a week among the farmers. The farmer revolt against mccarthyism was growing in direct ratio to the increasing severity of the dairy crisis. Back in 1952, when dairy prices were good, and things were booming in America's Dairyland—when Joe was picking on the Democrats—the farmers approved of keeping Joe in the Senate. But in early 1954 dairy surpluses were piling up, dairy prices were skidding, and Joe was picking on Republicans. The dairy farmers were in no mood for gags, especially if their industry and their political party were the victims.

Joe must have been aware of these rumblings from the Wisconsin grass roots, audible even in Texas where he basked in mild sunshine while disgruntled Wisconsin farmers wallowed through spring snowdrifts, grimly producing milk faster than the world wanted to drink it. Under the Texas sun Joe yawned, and uttered his astounding statement that the Wisconsin farmers should be paid 110 per cent of parity. This was a most interesting theory which would result in the federal government owning all the butter, since no consumer could afford to buy a pound of it.

The Wisconsin dairy farmer was in no mood to be kidded. He was ready to sign a petition, but how were we to get petitions to him?

The most logical solution seemed to be a "family size" petition in the rural newspapers of the state. But this was a $15,000 project, and we didn't have $15,000.

We did hit an unexpected jackpot of funds from Los Angeles, where the *Daily News* conducted an extensive and stirring fund-raising campaign. Without such help we were receiving small donations in considerable numbers from New York. We decided to visit New York and Washington, D. C., for two purposes:

1. To raise money for the newspaper petition project;
2. To assure my Republican friends that we hadn't gone off our rocker, and that the recall did have a chance of success.

The curse of "foreign money" did not greatly alarm me. Mccarthyism was a national, not a local, problem. Besides, McCarthy had taken the curse off "foreign money" by his

gleeful acceptance of large and well-publicized funds from
his wealthy Texas admirers.

Joe had one striking advantage in his sources of revenues. His money came from a few wealthy sources in
large chunks; ours came in small amounts from thousands
of "little people." A half-dozen telephone calls could
replenish Joe's "war chest." Ours was a laborious, time-
consuming project.

Early one Wednesday morning at the Madison, Wisconsin, airport Ivan Nestingen and I sat uneasily in a North
Central airlines plane as it headed eastward into murky,
threatening skies.

After a half century of anonymity, I confess I was more
than a little flattered at the recognition of the steward, the
pilots, and the passengers. Fame, no matter how fragile
and undeserved, has certain compensations.

A toy manufacturer across the aisle introduced himself,
and offered financial help to the recall.

"We're thinking of bringing out a new McCarthy talking doll," he confided, not too seriously, I assumed. "It's
going to say: 'I hate everybody who doesn't agree with
me. I'm full of deceit. I'm America's only 100 per cent
American!'"

A middle-aged attorney from New York sat in the
seat beside me. He finally closed the book he was reading
—a paper-bound who-dunnit.

"I'm an Irish Catholic," he said. "McCarthy's methods
disturb me, but I've considered his purposes to be praise-
worthy. I largely let the Church decide questions of morality for me. I gathered that Cardinal Spellman's statement

was a moral endorsement that the end justifies the means.
I guess I won't change my mind until the clergy makes
mccarthyism a moral issue."

I wondered what effect the speech of Bishop Sheil a
few days later had on the Irish attorney, but I didn't see
him again to find out.

Ivan and I landed at LaGuardia Field without advance
notice. We registered at the Biltmore Hotel, where we had
reservations. Then began the most hectic eighty hours of
my long and heretofore unexciting residence upon this
zany planet.

Within two hours we had been booked for three radio
appearances, two television filmings, and the New York
newspapers were acutely aware of our presence.

The first reporter to reach my room was tall, lean,
capable Ted Posten of the New York *Post*. Ted is sharp
as a new razor blade. We understood why he is held in
such high esteem in his trade. We'd hoped to see Jimmy
Wechsler, Ted's boss, and one of McCarthy's favorite
victims. Jimmy, frankly and honestly, was once a Communist. He reformed with a devastating vengeance which
makes him the most thoroughly hated of the anti-Communist fighters. But he wasn't willing to swap Communism for mccarthyism. In Joe's book only those reformed
Communists who support Joe are honest and effective.
This is an amazing and dangerous test of character, but
it's Joe's test, and it's one of his favorite weapons against
those who disagree with him. We talked with Jimmy over
the telephone, but he was catching a plane for Chicago,
and we were greatly disappointed.

That evening we split a radio program with two atomic
bomb experts on the cultured radio show capably emceed
by George Hamilton Coombs. One of the atomic experts
was quite concerned lest he become involved in the Mc-
Carthy issue, but Mr. Coombs is master of the art of
separation. We kept out of each other's hair.

At 1:30 A.M. we had an appointment on the Barry Gray
show. Fulton Lewis has called Barry a "left-winger." Personally we wouldn't have the faintest idea of what direction Mr. Gray pursues politically. We wouldn't know
whether he's white, pink, or crimson in his philosophy.
We're pretty sure he isn't green.

Barry Gray is a most amazing young man. His program
was not only unrehearsed, it was as full of surprises as a
chorus girl's diary. Barry's spot was midnight to 3 A.M., as
we recall it. Far down the corridor we chatted with
Arthur Godfrey's sister, another guest on Barry's program.
She was a little nervous awaiting her "ordeal." Apparently,
she got the full quota of nervousness for the Godfrey
family.

Over the public-address system we heard Barry interview her.

At 1:48 A.M.—Mr. Gray broadcast for three solid hours
without relaxing, and apparently without a time schedule
—we were hastily summoned. Short of breath after our
spirited dash, we were greeted by Mr. Gray's warm hand-
clasp. Simultaneously, he was introducing us to the radio
audience and asking us a question.

Barry was surrounded by coffeepots, cigarettes, and six

telephones. He talked without notes at a pace that made a tobacco auctioneer sound like he suffered speech impediment.

We kept wondering if anyone could be listening to radio at this unholy hour. Out in the cow country we go to bed when the milking is done. In New York, apparently, nobody ever goes to bed. The streets were still jammed with people when we left the studio. A radio was blaring in every taxicab and at every lunch counter. Barry Gray was still talking.

"I have two commercials," he was saying. "The first is, be sure to send as many bucks as you can afford to Joe Must Go, Sauk City, Wisconsin."

Only Wall Street was like a city of tombs within a city. Not a single pedestrian disturbed its sleeping calm. A thin, frustrated cat shuffled along a marble wall, meowing pitifully. If he found a mouse where he was prowling, his prey would surely be equipped with carborundum teeth.

There was a heartening, untidy stack of messages under our door at the Biltmore Hotel. The telephone was ringing steadily. We finally asked the operator to shut us off briefly at 5:45 A.M. We slept soundly until seven, when the phone began ringing again.

Bright and early we appeared upon the breakfast program of Tex and Jinx. Tex McCrary and his charming wife Jinx Falkenburg are delightful people who rib each other, their guest, and their audience through a swift half-hour of news and comment. In the *Star* each week I write a column which reports the strange, funny, and sometimes serious things that happen to my neighbors in my home

town. I call this back-yard gossip column "Star Dust." Tex
and Jinx had dug up one of the zaniest paragraphs somewhere. It was about worms. What it had to do with mccarthyism I'll never know, being thoroughly unsubtle, but
they made me read it to the radio audience unrehearsed.
I've never had any doubts since about the enduring qualities of the New York radio audience.

Tex directed publicity for the Republican party during
the last presidential campaign. He also wrote a sprightly
introduction to a popular book *Eisenhower—Man of the
Hour.* Coombs did a similar publicity stint for the Democratic party. Barry Gray, as I previously observed, has been
described in various shades of pink by Fulton Lewis, but I
have never relied on Mr. Lewis as an authority on such
matters. Whether the tempest I stirred up in New York
was deserved or undeserved, no one can deny that it was
strictly non-partisan.

By 9:30 A.M. Room 303 at the Biltmore was a madhouse.
A typical half-hour period was thus described by Robert
W. Wells, the New York representative of the Milwaukee
Journal, in the Sunday edition of his newspaper:

"Room 303 of the Biltmore hotel is located several hundred
yards from the lobby of Grand Central Station, but the re-
semblance between the two Saturday was striking, except
that the hotel room seemed more hectic.

"Leroy Gore, the Sauk City (Wis.) newspaper editor who
is executive secretary of the Joe Must Go club, and Ivan Nestingen, Madison attorney who is secretary of the same organization, checked into 303 Wednesday afternoon.

"The chaos has been abuilding ever since. What with New

Yorkers hammering on the door to leave contributions, to shake hands, or, occasionally, to argue—not to mention the constant jangle of the telephone—the visitors are convinced that Senator McCarthy is as much an issue here as he is back home.

"The Joe Must Go club representatives are here to help gain financial and moral support for the organization's drive for 403,804 signatures on petitions demanding McCarthy's recall from the Senate.

"In local radio and television appearances Gore and Nestingen have been pointing out to New Yorkers that contributions are welcome if addressed to 'Joe Must Go, Sauk City, Wisconsin,' and that about $15,000 is needed for expenses, including the buying of space in 350 Wisconsin papers for petitions which readers could sign. However, a lot of New Yorkers have been calling in person, rather than relying on the mails.

"The reporter kept notes of a typical half-hour in room 303. In summary—leaving out a lot of extraneous calls and comings and goings—it went like this:

"3 P.M.—A knock at the door. A well-dressed man who said he was from New York University shook Nestingen's hand, wished him well, said he'd left a contribution at the desk downstairs.

"3:01—Telephone rang. A woman reported she'd mailed a check to Sauk City.

"3:04—Gore got back from a long chat at the Harvard Club —with some Harvard grads—advertising men and bankers— who'd promised to mail checks. He started returning some of the most vital calls that had come in his absence.

"3:10—A reporter from the New York *Times* showed up. So did Mr. and Mrs. Merrill Gross of Cincinnati. Gross and his wife are vacationing in New York. When they heard of Gore's visit they dropped by to volunteer their help and were put to work answering the phone. Gross said he was an industrial engineer.

"3:14—A well-dressed woman, about 40, knocked at the door, said she was Mrs. Harding and wanted to ask Gore questions. It turned out she was an ardent admirer of McCarthy.

"3:20—A middle-aged woman came in with a $5 bill she said she wanted to give to the fund. Someone phoned from the lobby, was told he could come up if he didn't mind standing —all the chairs were filled.

"3:24—A bellboy brought up a contribution addressed to 'the publisher of the paper from the little town in Wisconsin.'

"3:27—A man in a gray suit came in, said he was from radio station WMGM and that 'the boys' had taken up a collection. He gave Gore the $20, said he wished it were more.

"3:30—Telephone rang again—it had been ringing almost constantly—a man informed Mrs. Gross he was mailing a contribution. There was a knock at the door. Another contributor. Gore turned to the man from the *Times,* whose note pad was still bare, and spread his arms apologetically.

" 'I'm awfully sorry,' he said. 'All these interruptions. But you see how it is.'

"And that's the way it has been, from the time New York residents found out about the two visitors from Wisconsin. Only by asking the hotel switchboard to cut off calls after 4 A.M. have they been able to get any sleep.

"The contributions that have been coming in here have been mostly $1.00 bills. The more substantial gifts to the fund —together with additional smaller ones—are being sent directly to Sauk City, Gore said.

" 'I think we've accomplished our purpose here,' he said. 'I feel we're going to get a healthy financial response.'

"Gore left Saturday afternoon for Washington. He will fly

back to Wisconsin Tuesday, he said. Meanwhile, he'll try to see as many of his old friends in the Republican party as he can.

" 'I want to enlist their support,' he said before he left. 'And I also want to let them know that I haven't become some kind of a crackpot and that I still am well aware that I'm just a small frog from a small puddle—and quite content to be just that.

" 'But this response we're getting here—it's really something, isn't it?' "

Mr. and Mrs. Gross spent most of their vacation serving as able secretaries for the Joe Must Go movement. Mr. Gross is an Ohio Young Republican chairman. He and his wife handled the throngs with speed and courtesy. They drafted time schedules, they saw that I ate with some regularity, and they even insisted that I get some sleep now and then. Since Ivan was forced to return to his law practice in Wisconsin, I sometimes shudder at what might have happened to me in New York if Mr. and Mrs. Gross had not appeared.

We left the room briefly at noon, in the capable hands of Paul Steiner, who was later to fly out to Wisconsin and offer his services as office manager. I was guest of honor at the "wedding anniversary" luncheon of Merrill and Ann Gross. I felt like an intruder, but they insisted on my presence. We ate exciting French food at an exciting French restaurant.

After midnight things weren't so pleasant in Room 303. Cranks and crackpots jammed the telephone lines. Typical were those who sneered:

"You'll never get out of New York with your ill-gotten money. We're coming up to take care of you."

Many of the calls were punctuated by profanity, obscenity, and even more specific threats. The hotel management and the house officer became so alarmed that they placed a lady with a telephone in full view of our door, with instructions to summon an officer in the event of trouble. Only two characters, however, made good their threat, and they were so inebriated that they presented no great problem. The house officer, however, was sure that his precautions were wise.

"These New York characters aren't like those you find out in Wisconsin," he warned me. "They mean what they say. I know some of them by reputation."

Somebody brought in an amusing clipping from Barry Gray's column in the *Post*. Barry is a great hand for tearing you down and building you up in the same sentence. He wrote:

"A little guy who looks like Casper Milquetoast, but who talks and acts like Jack the Giant Killer, blew into Manhattan Thursday for a series of money-raising meetings that're calculated to sever McCarthy's political ties with Wisconsin. . . . During our broadcast a woman phoned in to scream over the phone: 'That man talks like a damn' Communist.' Gore, a lifelong Republican, just laughed."

Compared with Barry's Casper Milquetoast simile, maybe the Kentucky Baptist who said I looked like a Methodist was just an old flatterer after all.

I shall always remember New York as the city in which

I had my first conversation with a real live Communist. I sought his name and telephone number from a newspaper friend of mine to ask one question:

"You Communists pretend to be enemies of McCarthy. Yet you do everything in your power to sabotage every reasonable movement to defeat him. You appear at meetings. You embarrass anti-McCarthy groups at every opportunity. Why?"

He laughed. "Apparently you misunderstand our purposes. Certainly we are bitter about McCarthy. He calls us names and even Communists do not like to be called names. But we are not opposed to mccarthyism. Mccarthyism is the thing which will tear your democracy apart because it breeds hate and distrust and prejudice, and democracy cannot survive except in an atmosphere of trust and harmony. The trouble is, human nature just isn't honest or trustworthy. McCarthy is proving it. When mccarthyism disappears something else will take its place. And ultimately mccarthyism or one of its successors will destroy you."

By Saturday I had dined at the Harvard Club, I had received the official blessing of a number of good men and true from Yale, I had been lost twice in the awesome complexities of Grand Central Station, and I had slept less than eight hours in three nights.

New York, I had decided, was quite a village, definitely full of people.

THE ONE MINUTE

I DIDN'T GET ...

I was a little jittery as I boarded the train for Washington. The immediate cause of my jitters was the partially inebriated gentleman in the seat across from me who kept toying with a bulky object in his coat pocket, and muttering:

"Them goddam Reds. . . . Them goddam Reds."

I was a little nervous about his intentions until the train paused at Baltimore, whereupon he staggered to his feet, leaned over my seat, and said:

"Them Cincy Reds couldn't beat the Des Moines Bloomer Girls softball team, could they?"

I hadn't the faintest idea whether they could or not, but it seemed safer and simpler to agree with him. I hope the Cincinnati fans will forgive me.

Highly pleased with my answer, the wobbly gentleman pulled the bulky object from his coat pocket. It was a bar guide.

"Take it," he said. "Ain't none of 'em any good. I tried 'em all and they just made me drunk."

A patient young reporter and a not-so-patient cameraman from the Washington *Post* were awaiting my arrival at the Burlington Hotel. I was an hour late, and the two of them were probably on double overtime, which doubtless did little to enhance my popularity with the financial office of the *Post*.

The Burlington was friendly and comfortable, but Sunday I moved to the Statler, where I had been registered in by friends before my arrival. I found a note under my door from Drew Pearson. He wanted me to have lunch with him.

I had anticipated that the extravagant attentions of the press, radio, and TV would eventually get under the thick hides of the apologists for mccarthyism, and that they'd administer some kind of an antidote. My only curiosity was the direction from which they might strike. I didn't have long to wait.

Fulton Lewis, Mutual's big noise, was publicly shocked at the discovery that I probably had a shabby past, and the recall movement was a phony anyway.

Stealing a page from Joe McCarthy's book, I wired Tom

O'Neil, president of the Mutual Broadcasting System, that Lewis had gone beyond news commentary into the field of political commentary, and I wanted equivalent time, under the terms of the federal communications act, to answer his personal attack.

I didn't get what I asked for, but Monday night Lewis continued his emotional attack and challenged me to appear upon his Tuesday-night program as a guest, to be dismembered by himself and his assistants Hurley and Cooper. I heard the radio challenge at the Cosmo Club, where I was dining with some new-found Washington friends. My first reaction was to laugh it off. The prospect of one country lamb being slaughtered by three city butchers did not appeal to me.

Late that night I appeared on the Federation of Labor newscast of Frank Edwards. In the corridor Bob Hurley, Fulton Lewis' No. 1 bat boy, needled as only the well-nourished and suave Bob Hurley can needle a guy. I began to simmer. Sure, I was a country jerk and I knew it. Out on the home lot I wouldn't poke fun at Mr. Hurley's inability to milk a cow. I saw no good reason why he should publicly rib me for lack of proficiency in his racket. The pot boiled over. I extended my stay in Washington a day, and knocked the chip off Mr. Lewis' shoulder. Not until two hours later, during the latter stages of digesting the thick steak sandwich I'd gnawed in the company with husky Frank Edwards at an all-night stand, did I get scared.

Mostly I don't scare easy, but this time I was really scared. I called a press conference. The scribblers turned out almost unanimously. They wrote their stories precisely as I'd have written the story. They said Mr. Lewis apparently thought it would be necessary to marshal three experts against one country editor from Wisconsin.

Among the impressive stack of messages were two telegrams from the boys at the coffee counter back home. Why waste your time with dull and uninspired characters like Mr. Lewis when the real experts on national and international problems meet every morning at ten back in the old home town, they wanted to know. I felt better, but I was still scared stiff.

I don't know how a guy feels waiting to be hung that night, but it couldn't be much worse than this. I couldn't reach Mr. Lewis, but I talked by phone with Mr. Hurley. Bob Hurley, I understand, is a self-made man, and very proud of his work, too. I asked for two things:

1. A script of the Friday and Monday night Lewis programs so I could get a clear picture of his complaints against me;

2. One minute on the program to state my position on mccarthyism.

I got neither.

It's only a couple of blocks from the Statler to the Mutual studio, but that was the longest walk of my life. Cameramen were waiting in the studio, but Mr. Lewis hadn't yet arrived. When he did arrive, I was immensely pleased to observe that he was as scared as I was. Maybe more so. I don't know what he expected—probably a Paul Bunyan with a sharp ax on his shoulder. The cameramen took some pictures, and I got over being scared. This guy

didn't look any tougher than Doc Bachhuber and John
Semrad, a couple of rugged Democrats back home.

Mr. Cooper was absent. Mr. Hurley was on the premises, but Mr. Lewis assured me he was there merely for his
scenic value. Mr. Lewis was prepared to take me on alone,
which was quite a concession, I gathered. I had a fiend-
ishly gleeful hunch that maybe the ribbing he'd taken at
the hands of the eastern newspapers might have had
considerable to do with his decision. He did drag Hurley
into the conversation, but only briefly and not too effectively. Here's how our radio conversation went:

LEWIS: Now, Mr. Gore, first of all, I'd like to ask you why
it was that you figured that you were entitled to time on
the air in response.

ME: I felt that you had gone beyond the realm of fair
news commentary into the field of politics.

LEWIS: All right, sir. Do you tend to give Senator Mc-
Carthy and his side of the picture equal space in your
newspaper?

ME: I think we do. As a matter of fact, for a number of
years I accorded him a great deal more space because I
supported him.

LEWIS: In the present series do you think your newspaper has devoted the same amount of time—this is trivial,
but interesting—I want you to understand, sir, that you
will be questioned here tonight only by me. I saw an article
in the United Press ticker this afternoon, stating that you
were going to be questioned not only by me, but by my
assistants. Because of the lateness of the hour of your ac-

ceptance, it was impossible to get one of them here from Chicago. Anyway, Mr. Hurley is here in the studio, but only I will ask you the questions. Now, as I understand it from Mr. Hurley, you told him last night that you were not going to accept this invitation. Why?

ME: That was my first reaction. I felt that one country boy going up against three pros would be an unequal battle, but I changed my mind. I decided maybe you were a good American and I am, too, and we are both fighting fundamentally for the same thing.

LEWIS: Don't worry about a pro. I'm sure you'll be able to take care of yourself perfectly all right. You changed your mind this morning, is that right?

ME: Yes.

LEWIS: Would you mind telling us, sir, about the collection of money for this? Where did the money come from to finance your trip to the East? Was that out of the fund?

ME: The money came out of my pocket.

LEWIS: Do you know, sir, how much you have gotten in the way of signatures to your petition thus far?

ME: The other day before I left we had approximately 185,000 signatures. We had 85,000 in our possession in the office.

LEWIS: Now who suggested to you, sir, that you go to New York?

ME: I think it was my idea.

LEWIS: Did you discuss it with other people?

ME: Oh, yes, quite a number.

LEWIS: Did you discuss this article of yours with any other people in advance of the time that you published it in your newspaper? The reason I ask that, to be perfectly fair, sir, is that I believe you told Mr. Hurley that the very same day that it was published in your newspaper it appeared also, or stories about it appeared also, in several of the Wisconsin newspapers.

ME: That's right, for the reason that we carry a Thursday publication date on our newspaper, even though we actually publish Wednesday evening.

LEWIS: And by Thursday it's your theory that it had gotten to the newspapers——

ME: It's only twenty-six miles from Sauk to Madison. The *Star* could have got down there that same night.

LEWIS: Have you had any conversation with Mr. William Evjue on this matter?

ME: Until two weeks ago Mr. William Evjue took a very dim view of this whole thing. No, I didn't consult with him beforehand for an obvious reason. This is the first time Bill and I have ever seen eye to eye on anything.

LEWIS: Are you familiar, sir, with an article that appeared in one of the Washington newspapers yesterday— an interview with you? "The originator of 'Joe Must Go' is confident that Joe will." The reason I ask you this is whether you were correctly quoted in all of this. Here I see you quoted as telling a story about going to the home of a friend, and the little girl sitting up on your lap and asking if the United States' government were run by lies, and that that inspired you to start this "Joe Must Go" campaign.

ME: I haven't read the story, but I think that is essentially correct. I recall telling the reporter that.

LEWIS: The reason I ask you this is because we want to

clear up some confusion because Mr. Bob Hurley reports otherwise on the reason that you told him. Bob, would you give your——

HURLEY: General Zwicker report.

LEWIS: Mr. Hurley said you were outraged at the testimony and handling of the Zwicker case, and that that was the thing that touched you off on this "Joe Must Go" campaign.

ME: I also told Mr. Hurley that the Mrs. Moss case was a factor in it. Those were all factors, but the moment I changed my mind was described in the story you just referred to.

LEWIS: Now, sir, have you ever read the Zwicker testimony?

ME: I think so.

LEWIS: In its entirety?

ME: I read what was published in the metropolitan dailies in our area.

LEWIS: But you didn't read the entire testimony—you just read stories about the testimony?

ME: It is my recollection that they were represented to be the full text.

LEWIS: Did you ever read the Peress testimony?

ME: No.

LEWIS: —on which that was based?

ME: There are a lot of things I haven't read, Fulton, but let's confine ourselves to the issue. I have found a lot to admire in Joe McCarthy. I supported him for a long time, but there are several very simple reasons why I now oppose him, and I think in view of the fact that you have five opportunities a week to tell why you are pro-McCarthy that you should yield this final minute to discussing why I am anti-McCarthy.

LEWIS: Well, sir, I'm delighted. I wanted to ask you one more question.

ME: All right.

LEWIS: We have just a moment left. This newspaper article reports that you stated that all but six papers in the state of Wisconsin are with your cause—the anti cause. Now, I happen to have here a telegram from Ellsworth Coe, editor of the Whitewater *Register,* immediate past president of the Wisconsin Press Association, in which he says, "If Mr. Gore says all but six papers are with him, he should hurry home for a recount." What comment would you have on that?

ME: We get a great many Wisconsin rural papers on our exchange list. As far as I knew when I made that statement, only six opposed us. That's what I said.

LEWIS: All right, sir. Thank you very much. That's the top of the news as it looks from here.

Next morning's newspapers summed up the interview thus: "The country editor from Wisconsin didn't get the one minute he asked for on Fulton Lewis' program last night."

I consulted briefly with farm and industrial leaders, and received cheering assurances of support. The assurances were a little more optimistic than the performance, but that is neither here nor there.

Meantime, things had been happening back in Wiscon-

sin. The Madison *Capital Times* had voiced strong editorial support of the recall. The Milwaukee *Journal*
wouldn't go quite that far; while they had warmly endorsed the purposes of the movement, they wouldn't
get involved as one of its backers. They were willing to
put on a bathing suit, but they hesitated to get it wet.

The top brass in the labor unions took about the same
position. They'd be delighted no end if it worked, but
until we could show them a blueprint of success they
wanted no official part in it. The separate unions and the
little guy in the shop worked hard and long, but the top
leadership stayed on the side lines. They'd cheer for us,
but they weren't making any tackles or throwing any
blocks for the halfbacks.

In Washington I talked with three senators and a con-
gressman representing both political parties. One of them
sneaked out to meet me at an out-of-the-way restaurant.
Another almost had a heart attack when I showed up at
his office. Two of them met me down in the basement to
avoid popping flash bulbs.

Their reasons were plausible enough. They couldn't
help us, they contended, by identifying themselves with
the recall, and they might discount their own capacity for
public service. Once anyone in public life comes out
against McCarthy, apparently, he gets buried in an
avalanche of mail, and his office gets nothing done except
to deal with the cranks and crackpots. All of them recognized the frightening danger in mccarthyism, but they
didn't want to be quoted.

I suspect there were deeper reasons. Olin Miller said it

once: "God help the rich. The poor can sleep on fire escapes."

Only the little people, apparently, can stand a lost cause once in a while. They haven't much to lose.

Before I left the Mutual studios, a lady telephoned. She identified herself as Eleanor Lenroot, wife of the late Senator Lenroot. She invited me to her apartment for a late dinner of Virginia ham and quite a few other choice groceries. I accepted. The Lewis ordeal had so disturbed me I'd missed two meals consecutively, and missing meals is not one of my favorite weaknesses.

Mrs. Lenroot was furious. Her husband was a senator in the days when honesty and dignity were in style. McCarthy, she told me, had neither.

"My husband warned me the first day this man came to the Senate that he'd be a troublemaker," she recalled. "He was too brash. If you haven't got dignity and honor, you haven't got anything."

A week later she announced it to the world. She also met Joe McCarthy coming out of the Senate hearing room and told him to his face. The story didn't get the newspaper play it merited. I asked some of the scribblers about it. They had a weird notion she was senile. Phooie! If any two of them started to follow her at 7 A.M. their tongues would be hanging over their chin by eleven. If this be senility, then what the world needs is lots more senility.

I lunched and talked with Drew Pearson at the Cosmo Club. He's a tall, swift, slender man who yields only partially to the march of time. He looks like he might be sixty; he walks like he's sixteen. He was interested in the recall's prospects of sucess, but more interested in its annoyance index.

"Joe bloats with pride when a senator attacks him, so long as they pronounce his name right. But he can't fight a half-million voters in Wisconsin."

Somehow he reminded me of Lewis C. French of the Milwaukee *Journal,* which is a great compliment to Pearson since I personally consider Lew to be the greatest reporter I've ever known. Pearson speaks in the same close-clipped, emotionless voice, he eats with the same precise efficiency, chewing each bite the recommended number of times, as though eating were a purely functional activity. He didn't even lift his voice as he described how Joe had slugged him in the washroom of the Senate building. Joe, apparently, chooses his foes in fisticuffs with the same care as he does in the committee room.

But it wasn't McCarthy's physical violence Pearson fears. It's the ruthless capacity of the man and the Evil Ism he has created to smash the lives and the souls of those who dare lift a voice against him.

As the giant stratoliner swept upward and westward toward home, I looked back at the nation's capital. But a dark, scowling face kept blotting out the golden reflections from the capitol dome, and a petulant nasal voice kept drowning out those heart-warming words: ". . . Land of the free, and home of the brave."

I had found little of bravery against this newest and

perhaps gravest threat to our freedom. Washington would face the Red hordes without flinching, but Washington trembled before one man equipped only with a slashing tongue and a soul saturated with deceit.

200 PERCENT

AMERICANISM . . .

An excited reporter met my plane at the Chicago airport.

"Fulton Lewis says 200 business and professional men are meeting you at the village limits, armed with petitions to 'Give the Door to Gore.' What do you think?"

After the initial shock, my first reaction was that the home town must have grown considerably during my absence, since the Sauk-Prairie main streets boasted only 156 business and professional leaders at the moment of my departure. Sauk-Prairie were lively, growing villages, but it seemed to me a 20 per cent growth was too much to expect in a little more than a week.

The "Door for Gore" club was no great shock to me. A telegram delivered to me in Washington had warned that the frustrated restaurant owner had vowed he would drive me out of town. The remainder of the wire read:

LARGELY ONE MAN MOVEMENT WITH FOUR CONVERTS THEY SPLIT UP A THOUSAND PER CENT AMERICANISM FIVE WAYS GIVING EACH OF THEM TWO HUNDRED PER CENT.

In spite of this assurance, I was a little worried. In thirty years I'd managed to save $35,000. I had every cent tied up in the *Star,* plus a substantial $18,000 mortgage held by the Sauk City bank.

I had no real way of knowing whether Fulton Lewis' jubilant prediction of disaster was predicated on fraud or fallacy. I knew it wasn't completely true. In any community there are a few dull and misguided souls whose simple solution to all community problems is to drive out of the village precincts those who do not agree with them. But they were fairly scarce in Sauk-Prairie, unless I erred in judgment. Fulton Lewis' "special correspondent" was relaying a hope rather than a fact, I suspected.

On the last lap of my air journey home I was summoned from the plane in Madison to the local radio station for a broadcast. They were playing a transcription from the restaurant owner. His purpose, he said, was "to drive Gore and his movement from our peaceful villages before they cast an undesirable stigma upon us." He sounded more bitter than convincing. I predicted over the airways that Sauk-Prairie's sense of humor would swiftly reassert itself, and so would the Americanism that had kept the villages off the jagged rocks of bigotry for one hundred and forty years.

Back in Sauk City I discovered that the restaurant-mink ranch owner had been a busy little bee indeed during my absence.

To those who disliked me he boasted that his purpose was to drive me out of town. "You'd better find another job right quick," he told one of my printers after a bowling session one night.

To those who had nothing against me, but plenty against the recall movement, he piously pretended that I was a great guy, but his object was to relieve the village of this dastardly political movement.

He created a temporary tornado when he briefly persuaded the village president that the recall movement was driving most of the customers from main street. But, in the best tradition of vindictive agitators, he overplayed his hand. He made a great point of a purely fictitious story that a local dairy plant had lost its best wholesale customer because of the recall. The plant manager wasn't approached for a week after most of the main-street businessmen had swallowed the bait. No one, it seems, thought of asking him until a shoe merchant did. The dairy processor laughed. The story was pure fabrication. The restaurant-mink ranch owner created another minor tempest with a post card allegedly received from a tourist who threatened never again to stop in a Communist town like Sauk City. But the post card read too much like an advertisement. It didn't fool anyone very long. Besides, filling stations, restaurants, and taverns were reporting that hundreds of tourists were stopping every week, attracted by the national publicity of the Joe Must Go movement. The economic argument began to leak like a sieve.

Down at Madison the Door for Gore president keynoted a "For America" party rally. One reporter said it was attended by twenty-four party enthusiasts, three reporters, and five guys who came in to get out of the cold. The mink man said I'd come to Sauk "without enough money to buy hamburger," that I'd launched the recall to pay off my newspaper mortgage.

Next morning a half-dozen businessmen offered to buy my wife a hamburger when she went downtown on a shopping errand.

With considerable desk pounding, the mink man and a friend canceled their subscriptions to the *Star*. The friend sneaked back hastily to resubscribe, and the mink man seemed to know each week what went on in our news columns. At this point eight subscribers had canceled, and we'd gained forty-five.

How many signers the mink man got on his ouster petition will probably be a permanent mystery. Friends doubling as sleuths for us never found more than three signatures on one petition. We offered to run the petition without charge in the *Star*, but the mink man spurned the offer.

If there was any doubt that a heavier hand than the mink rancher was behind the Door for Gore movement, the mink rancher dispelled the doubt. Shortly thereafter the Door for Gore movement assumed considerably more stature than a mere local tempest in a teapot. It became part of a pattern to discredit me, discredit the movement, and to defeat this or future recall efforts by increasing the difficulties of getting signatures, circulators, and funds, and to consume the time and energies of the recall leadership. I quote from a news report in the Chicago *Sun-Times:*

". . . the counter-attack against the Joe Must Go movement became visible as pro-McCarthy forces went to work.

"In Sauk City, it took the form of a vigilante campaign to run Leroy Gore's Joe Must Go headquarters out of town.

"Organizer of the counter-movement is Roman Reuter, proprietor of Romie's Dinette and also operates a mink ranch.

"He set up his headquarters in the back room of Otto Lehman's saloon, overlooking the Wisconsin River. Just about every day . . . he gets stacks of mail from all over the nation.

"It includes commendations from the For America chapter in Madison, the Youth for McCarthy Club of Corpus Christi, Texas, and from Bradley R. Taylor of Rhinelander, assistant campaign director of the Republican National Committee.

"In the mail is a post card from Sleepy Eye, Minn., a religious tract from Los Angeles, a defense of McCarthy by the National Economic Council, and a four-page, anti-Semitic newspaper published in New Jersey.

"Reuter is president of the Door for Gore group. Other officers are Lehman, the saloonkeeper; Jack Hammerle, a nightclub owner; Elmer Ganser, who operates a dance hall; Royal Dickson, a garage man, and Merton Murphy, in the feed business.

"Reuter proudly displays a framed photo showing him walking beside Senator McCarthy in a Legion parade.

"It's kept safely behind the bar of Otto Lehman's tavern, but as soon as he gets time, Reuter plans to hang it in the back-room headquarters.

"The mink rancher says he has met McCarthy on three occasions since the Door for Gore campaign started and has received four letters from the senator commending his efforts."

The Sauk City Men's Club met Monday night, just two days and a month after my recall editorial had been published. President Jerome Lochner and Program Chairman W. J. Coenan had promised an open hearing. I wasn't afraid the Men's Club would vindicate the Door for Gore Club. I was afraid I might lose by winning. Feelings were running high. Small-town main streets have an unfortunate habit of choosing up sides on controversial subjects, and small-town newspapers can't afford to lose many friends among the advertisers. There aren't many advertisers, and the margin between profit and no profit is always a slender one. I don't recall that a small-town newspaperman has ever had his income tax investigated.

Al Davidson, Sauk-Prairie lumberman, former president of the Men's Club, and currently president of the Prairie du Sac Lions Club, offered a resolution of confidence in me. He submitted that the Reuter petitions in circulation, which requested only that the recall headquarters leave town, was not in harmony with the official name of the club—Door for Gore—that the club was obviously dedicated to my removal, and the petition tactics represented an obvious effort to confuse the issue.

Novelist August Derleth made quite a speech, including this paragraph:

"All men of good will owe the Door for Gore projectors and supporters a vote of thanks, for nothing any of us could do better illustrates just what it is we are fighting against, this evil thing that mccarthyism is, than the actions of the Door for Gore supporters. The fellow who beats his chest and tells you he is a 100 per cent pure American is entirely likely not to know what genuine Americanism is."

I didn't speak long. I didn't have to. I merely emphasized that I recognized the right of any citizen to be pro-McCarthy, but I hoped they recognized my right to be anti-McCarthy. "It is entirely true that this highly controversial issue may have caused some hard feelings in our village. But I suspect it has caused no more hard feelings than some of the ball games at the athletic park. To me it seems much healthier for people to get excited over politics than sports events."

The Men's Club unanimously adopted the Davidson resolution expressing confidence in me and welcoming to Sauk City any movement with a legal and democratic purpose.

William T. Evjue wrote in the *Capital Times* of Madison:

"Whatever its purpose, it [the Door for Gore Club] smacks alarmingly of vigilantism. Mr. Gore is directing a project that is entirely legal and democratic. He is following the constitutional and statutory provisions for the recall of a public official. He is acting according to American institutions and traditions.

"But what legal basis is there for such an organization as this Door for Gore Club if it is not intimidation to prevent a man from exercising a legal and wholly American right? Do we not see here the same extra-legal principles that motivated the Ku Klux Klan and other terroristic groups?

"What can this organization possibly do in a legal way to drive the recall headquarters of Leroy Gore out of Sauk City? They can, no doubt, make it difficult for him to function. They can burn fiery crosses on his lawn. They can smash the windows of his plant and home. They can paint his door yellow. They can do many of the things that were done by the KKK or the super-patriots of World War I who practiced their vigilantism against the so-called 'pro-Germans.'

"But they have no legal ground to stand on.

"Mr. Gore is finding out what's behind mccarthyism."

On that day signatures to recall petitions had reached approximately one half of the required legal total.

The Green Feather group at the University of Chicago asked me to speak. I appeared in historic Reynolds Hall. The Green Feather group, I was told, had its beginning when an Indiana librarian charged that Robin Hood and his followers were communistic because they took from the rich and gave to the poor. Promptly on most of the college and university campuses over the nation students began to wear green feathers as an intellectual protest.

They laughed with me when I described the circumstances following their invitation and my acceptance. Members of the Joe Must Go committee insisted that I check the organization for subversive traits. It seemed a little silly to me. As Woodrow Wilson once said: "Certainly the radicals won't convert me, and I might convert them."

This is another of the sad indictments against mccarthyism. There was once in free America a day when a good American could lift his voice where he chose, speak to those he chose to speak to, read the books and magazines he chose to read. Today, we are permitted to speak and read only as mccarthyism dictates we read and speak.

This, in part, is what I said at Chicago:

"Two weeks ago in New York City Senator McCarthy brushed me off with the comment that 'Anybody can make the headlines by calling McCarthy an s.o.b.'

"The senator is right. The senator probably knows more about the technique of making headlines than any man or woman of our generation. The senator made his headlines by calling Acheson, Truman, Marshall, Stevenson, and Eisenhower nasty names. The difference between us is this: I am fully aware that fame achieved by calling another man names is as phony as a three-dollar bill, and as fleeting and fragile as it is phony. The senator hasn't yet made that discovery.

"Whatever your convictions about McCarthy and mccarthyism, if you know anything about Communist hunting, you know this: barring an unlikely miracle, McCarthy has never caught a Communist and he never will. Even in those dark and best-forgotten days when I supported the senator I knew this. With the exception of the gullible, the cranks, and the fanatics, of which there are many, those rare McCarthy supporters among the reasonable people will admit it today. Senator McCarthy's sole asset to the nation is his constant re-emphasis of the Communistic threat.

"What price are we paying for this dubious asset?

"McCarthy's slanders against the armed forces have given the Russian propaganda mills the very opportunity they sought to picture America as a bickering, impotent nation. If there is a warmonger today, he is Senator McCarthy, whose reckless words have shattered the foundations of our cherished American institutions."

IT'S A

SMALL WORLD . . .

Americans are great hands at "grandstand quarterbacking." For years, from well up in the bleachers, I've been telling the quarterback what play to call next, the pitcher how to get that 3-2 strike ball in there, and the politician how to win his current campaign. I have now taken the cure. Hereafter, I'll keep my big mouth shut.

Approximately 25,000 citizens volunteered unsolicited advice during the ten weeks of the signature drive. Fine-type ideas they were, too. Most frequently they recommended that we hire circulators at maybe twenty cents a signature. Mathematically, this was a dilly. We'd hire 404 circulators to get 1,000 signatures each. We couldn't miss.

Except for the fact that it involved $80,000 we didn't have.

There was another excellent suggestion, considerably less expensive. It involved the mailing to every mail patron in the state a thorough exposé of the sad McCarthy record, accompanied by a family-size petition, and instructions for completion and mailing. The cost would have been approximately $15,000. Unfortunately, we didn't have $15,000 either.

Country editors, like country preachers, don't attach too much importance to money. After the help is paid Saturday night, if there are a few bucks in the till, we stick them into our jeans for the wife's shopping. If the till is empty, we shrug our shoulders resignedly, charge the week's groceries, and hope for better luck next Saturday.

I learned about money from the recall movement. You've got to have money to spend if you're running a recall. It costs money to rent typewriters, to get petitions, letterheads, and other office supplies printed. Postage costs money. If the postal department deficit is erased this year, the recall movement had quite a hand in it. At the last minute, when it appeared one great, jumbo-size effort might possibly put us over, we persuaded some competent citizens to leave their jobs and work for us as organizers. They were paid wages and expenses.

While most of our office help was volunteer help without salary, we did find it necessary to hire some help. The recall officers, who worked like dogs at considerable personal sacrifice in time and money, got expense money for extracurricular trips, but no wages.

We ran some ads in the big dailies, and bought some radio and television time. We were tighter with our funds than a No. 6 shoe on a No. 9 foot, but we managed to spend more than $25,000 of the $30,000 we collected. It's all in Treasurer Carl Lachmund's public report.

One of the most common complaints of friends and enemies was that I spent too much time out of Wisconsin. Actually, I spent ten and one-half days out of Wisconsin during the seventy days of the extended recall effort; slightly more than a week in New York and Washington; one and one-half days in Los Angeles; a half day in Buffalo; and a few hours in Chicago.

Thanks chiefly to generous backing by the Los Angeles *News*, we received almost a third of our funds from California and the L.A. area. Another third came from Chicago, New York, and the East.

That doesn't leave much from Wisconsin, does it? The explanation isn't that Wisconsin was unwilling to spend money to defeat McCarthy. But you must remember that some 6,500 citizens were spending time and money—considerable time and money—circulating petitions. Lots of them sent in a dollar or two, but dollars don't add up rapidly. We just didn't get any big money in this campaign. The big people were mostly afraid for various reasons. Only the little people had starch in their spines.

Personally, there isn't much of the gypsy in my soul. What I saw of New York was the inside of a real nice hotel room, the insides of several television and radio broadcasting rooms, the inside of Grand Central Station, and Wall Street at night. What I saw of Washington included four assorted senators and congressmen, two hotel rooms, a basement room in the Senate building, seven polite labor leaders, and more radio-television headquarters. I averaged three and one-half hours' sleep a night, and I came home dead tired with my ulcers bouncing like mad.

All my life I've wanted to see California—but not in thirty-six hours on a political mission. Every time I think of it, I have to take another vitamin capsule and a couple of aspirin tablets. Los Angeles is a lovely city, full of lovely people. Sometime I hope to meet them under circumstances more intelligible than running the tape backward at full speed in a tape recorder.

Sure, I went out of Wisconsin to raise funds. If I hadn't, the sheriff would have closed our office doors. I'm not sorry. I don't apologize. I am merely more grateful than I can put into words for the generosity of hundreds of patriotic citizens in many states who had sufficient faith in me and the movement I launched to invest their sweaty, hard-earned dollars in us.

Out of my dizzy, daffy, spinning recent past, I've managed to pluck these brief and fleeting memories:

Los Angeles

The world has indeed shrunk to the size of an orange when you can eat a late lunch in Chicago and an early dinner in Los Angeles.

I shall never quite forget the thrill when our big stratocruiser knifed through the thick, stubborn Los Angeles fog, right over the housetops of what TV commentator

Chet Huntley chooses to call "the many villages looking for a city."

It was early morning, and I was flattered and pleased when a burly gentleman, who introduced himself as a famed L.A. art dealer, met me at the airport gate. There had been no food on the plane, and I greedily gulped a tasty breakfast. It was cold and damp that April day in L.A., and I lamented my too-abundant faith in the L.A. Chamber of Commerce. I'd left my topcoat in Wisconsin.

But as we sped smoothly along well-kept streets, I marveled at the magic that had created this amazing city out of the desolate desert. Here I saw my first palm tree. With the patient aid of my host, I even learned to differentiate between the date palm and the other palms, a horticultural achievement which surpasses that of many natives to whom palm trees are as ho-hum as maples in Wisconsin.

Los Angeles is a city of appalling distances, and people like those back home. You've heard tell that the people are as artificial as the man-made city itself. They aren't. Even in Hollywood the most bizarre characters I saw were tourists from Iowa and Wisconsin trying to look like what a native Californian is supposed to look like. The people of L.A., like the people of Sauk City and Milwaukee, are too busy getting the work of the world done to engage in public theatrics.

Hollywood has more homely girls, probably, than any other city in the country. I make haste to add it also has more pretty girls. It has more girls, period.

I hate to disillusion you about Hollywood and Vine, but it's just an ordinary street corner. Hollywood has prettier street corners. So does your home town. I stood there for quite a while, but I didn't see Rita Hayworth, Lana Turner, or Clark Gable. All I saw was a gaudy model-A Ford full of Illinois G.I.'s who stopped to holler at me: "Whereinell's Hollywood and Vine?"

I have vague and kaleidoscopic memories of being whisked astounding distances in cars and taxis—or maybe it was Aladdin's magic carpet—of smiling at and speaking to innumerable warmhearted people, of shaking hands until I was sure my arm would fall off, and of eating vast quantities of excellent food.

I remember appearing on numerous broadcasts, of which the TV news show conducted by Chet Huntley was most memorable. At the conclusion of the show, the ventilating fan, clinging to the ceiling by rusty screws, grew weary at last and plummeted like an H-bomb onto my poorly protected dome. It raised a lump, but fortunately the safest place to hit a newspaperman is on his head. The fan was damaged, but I wasn't.

"You're the first guest I've had in a long time who brought down the house," said Mr. Huntley. "Usually they're courteous enough to leave that to me."

At the *News* I met a lady photographer, easy enough on the eyes to be in the movies. She'd been shoved down a flight of stairs by the "little mccarthyites of L.A.," and she'd escaped critical injuries by a miracle. I was a little ashamed of my complaints about my own puny political woes.

The Windy City

John Nuveen is one of the bravest men I've ever known.

I don't mean spectacular, physical bravery. There's quite another kind of bravery.

Nuveen is an investment broker. Obviously, a very able and successful investment broker. A tall, balding, distinguished-looking man, he impresses you with his air of quiet dignity. Here is a man endowed by the gods for a calm existence.

A small-town boy, I'm not accustomed to the impressive elegance of Mr. Nuveen's office. I'd heard of rugs with pile thick enough to bury your ankles, but I'd never before walked on one, even though my father was a furniture dealer.

We were joined by a half-dozen ladies of assorted ages. There was, however, a uniformity of charm and culture among them. They tried very hard and with considerable talent to make me feel at ease, but I regret to report that they did not succeed too well. There is nothing wrong with the newspaper trade, and there is nothing wrong with the guys and gals who patronize the ten-o'clock Kaffee Klatsch in my home town—nothing wrong with them that isn't wrong with the human race in general. But never before had I encountered culture in such copious quantities. I hope I behaved well. I was a little too flustered to remember whether I did or not.

I kept looking at Mr. Nuveen and these charming women, and I kept asking myself: "Why are they risking their quiet, well-ordered lives?"

I knew something of Mr. Nuveen's background. An Eisenhower Republican, like me, this was not the first time he had betrayed an aggressiveness that his manner didn't indicate. Yet I had a feeling his conviction was deeper than a political conviction. These people didn't talk about politics. If they hated McCarthy, they didn't say so. They merely talked about what mccarthyism was doing to public morality. Any one of them was much smarter than I. I'm sure they approved of what I was doing because to me the problem of mccarthyism is the same kind of impersonal moral problem it is to them, even though they can express that problem much better than I can express it.

It was a very proud moment when Mr. Nuveen agreed to serve as chairman of the Chicago committee.

Another memorable experience of my brief stay in Chicago, was when I shook hands with Bishop Sheil.

I am a Protestant, but Sauk City is the second community in which I have lived at peace with my mostly Catholic neighbors. I once did publicity chores for Father Flanagan when Boys Town was a fairly young and struggling institution. I regard Father Flanagan and Bishop Sheil as among the great Americans of my generation. I have the greatest respect for spiritual men who preach to those who are already saved. But Father Flanagan and Bishop Sheil have done their best work with those who are not saved, especially with the youth who have their years of good or bad achievement ahead of them. That, I think, is very important indeed.

Bishop Sheil is a kindly, bright-eyed man whose activity

would frighten many a man half his age. He feels very
keenly, as I do, that mccarthyism is more than a shabby
one-man show. Mccarthyism, unfortunately, is a symptom
of a dangerous state of mind—the same state of mind responsible for the Ku Klux Klan, Hitlerism, and Communism. The brazen egotism, the tendency of mccarthyism to
brand all those who do not subscribe without question to
its goals and its methods, all these could consume our liberties in a crisis which could occur at any moment.

But the measure of the man was this parting sentence:

"The true index of mankind isn't that so many have hate
in their hearts, but that they are so greatly outnumbered
by those who have decency and love in their hearts."

I split Irving Kupcinet's television show with a talented
young artist who had done a series of religious paintings
for a new edition of the Bible. Kup, who doubles as a col-
umnist for the *Sun-Times*, is a big, pleasant, rugged young
man with an easy TV manner. The trouble with TV is
the screen in front of you. Radio broadcasts I don't mind.
All you've got to worry about is how silly you may sound.
With television you've got to worry about how silly you
look, too. I kept looking at the screen and thinking of that
Kentucky Baptist. Maybe the guy's got a point.

Back in my hotel room, there was the usual parade of
anti-McCarthy visitors. I was especially pleased with a
delegation from the Railway Brotherhood, meeting in convention at the hotel. They were from many states, but "the
cowboys of the iron horses" are all great guys. I like them.

The beds and the available chairs were covered with visitors when a typical pro-McCarthy fan called. This guy had kind of a nice voice, but the stream of indecencies that issued from his lips called for a jumbo-size bar of Ivory soap to wash out his mouth. Two of the railroad men, who couldn't help overhearing since they were seated beside me, looked as though they'd just walked into the woman's shower room by mistake.

Here's a reasonable facsimile of the conversation, minus the indecencies:

ANONYMOUS: Get out of town, you Jew-loving Commie, #*!%* before us real Americans in Chicago fill you as full of holes as a Wisconsin cheese.

ME: I'd like to accommodate you, but at the prices they charge here I can't afford to pay for a room I don't sleep in.

ANONYMOUS: You won't get out of town alive with that money you hijacked out of the Chicago Reds. Where did your family come from? Israel?

ME: No, although I wouldn't be ashamed of it if they did. They came from England.

ANONYMOUS: (triumphantly): Just as I thought! The English are almost as bad as the Jews, you English #*!%*! Take your blankety-blank family back to London where you belong.

ME: Sorry, but my folks came over in 1774. They're beginning to like it here, and I doubt if I could persuade them to leave.

(A long pause.)

ANONYMOUS: Say, whatinell's the matter with you, anyway? You don't sound like a bad guy. Who's hoodwinked you into fighting Joe who's fighting the Commies?

ME: You don't sound like a bad guy either. Just a confused guy. Someday you'll come out from under the anaesthetic like I did, and you'll wonder why it took you so long.

ANONYMOUS: The hell I will!

(Bang!)

Another interesting caller was a psychiatrist who confided that a local mental institution where he practiced had just admitted the first patient obsessed with the notion that he was David Schine.

"Fame," he said, "has come to Schine at last."

At 10 P.M. George Harris called. George is a character who writes for *Time* magazine. George is handy with words.

"How about a sandwich?" he suggested.

Since I hadn't taken nourishment since 12:15 P.M., this impressed me as a real good idea. I said so.

"See you in forty-five minutes," George promised.

I wasn't told until later that Harris, in spite of his multiple talents, has never learned to tell time. Fortunately, on this occasion his wife accompanied him, and she was approximately as hungry as I. George called from the lobby, and the following intellectual conversation took place:

GEORGE: Come on down.

ME: A fine-type idea. But having never seen each other, how do you propose to recognize me? With three national conventions on the premises, probably 1,500 citizens will be waiting for the elevator. Maybe *Time* reporters are psychic.

(A slight pause, punctuated by the grinding of the gears of George's massive mental machinery.)

GEORGE: Put a pencil in your teeth. I'll put one in mine. I betcha no one else will think of that.

They didn't. But neither did either of us anticipate how silly we'd look and feel walking out among 1,500 people with a pencil clutched firmly in our bicuspids. I spotted him right away, and vice versa. We laughed so hard we nearly swallowed the pencils. Nobody else laughed. They merely looked scared as hell, all 1,500 of them. Mrs. Harris didn't look scared. She hadn't been married to George too long, but long enough to get used to him, I guess. She just shook her head as we galloped toward the door.

Next morning I packed my toothbrush and called the Nuveen office. His secretary was quite excited. Since the news had come out in the Chicago newspaper that Mr. Nuveen was heading the Chicago fund drive, he'd had quite a few telephone calls. Most of them approved. A few anonymous callers recommended shipping him to Moscow. His secretary didn't think Mr. Nuveen would be interested. Business was too good in Chicago, and he'd miss the lake view from his window.

Buffalo

All I knew about Buffalo was the song about the guy who was shuffling off to there in three melodious verses.

On the plane I encountered a young fellow from the University of Wisconsin campus. He was en route to Niagara Falls job hunting. Without urging, he confided that this was his first plane trip, he was thrilled to pieces—but not so thrilled about the McCarthy recall movement.

Probably his thinking on the recall subject was perfectly clear to him, but it confused me considerably. It seems he was opposed to the recall "because those young A.D.A.s on the campus are pushing it. They're a very brazen outfit."

His logic seemed to be that, while mccarthyism was about the same kind of blessing as double pneumonia, the U. of W. Young Republicans were going to be for it as long as the young Democrats were against it. Logic, I gathered, is no more of an epidemic in the rising generation than it was in my generation.

Frankly, I'm not much of an authority on Buffalo. I got no farther than the late-lunch counter tavern a block and a half away where they serve Milwaukee beer and Madison hot dogs. They also watch fights on television.

The Greater Buffalo Advertising Club, I was told, is the world's largest luncheon club. I can believe it. The hungry members jammed tables in the three-level dining room, and spilled over to "standing room only" around the edges.

One of the committee told me it was the largest audience since Knute Rockne spoke there. Probably most of them wished they'd eaten a cheeseburger at an automat. As an orator, I rank somewhere between Alf Landon and a novice Fuller Brush salesman making his first demonstration.

The only story I have to tell compares with dried-beef gravy as a topping for raspberry ice cream. I start out apologizing for my long support of Senator McCarthy. Then I flip like a pancake on a griddle, expressing vast wonderment that the whole world doesn't flip with me.

Maybe they don't adore me in Green Bay, but I got the impression they love me in Buffalo. A Young Republican jumped up to assure me that I shouldn't judge the New York G.O.P. infants by the Young G.O.P. in Wisconsin. They classed McCarthy with lumbago, hungry hornets, and poison oak.

The members wrote questions on slips of paper and sent them up to the speakers' table. Very good questions, too. One of the most popular was whether the hearings would adjourn in time for Senator Mundt to make a scheduled appearance before the club early in June. I didn't think so. I'm very proud of this prediction. To the best of my recollection, it's the first time I've ever made a successful political prediction.

WHO'S AFRAID

OF THE BIG, BAD

WOLF? . . .

For almost a generation a quiet "industrial revolution" has been going on in Wisconsin and other agricultural states. This revolution is about to exert a significant influence upon Wisconsin politics, just as it already has had a significant impact upon Wisconsin economics.

One of the most pitiful men I know was a national corn-husking champion of the 1920's. That was back in the days when we used to "snap" corn in the fall directly from the stalk, husk it neatly, and throw it into the wagon alongside, pulled by a team of well-educated horses.

This acquaintance lives in a very dead and almost forgotten past. His friends are often embarrassed in his company. Cameras and flash bulbs still excite him after thirty years, just as the aging fire horse out in the pasture is still thrilled to the brink of a heart attack by the sound of the siren. Ordinarily a conservative and well-behaved gentleman, he has no hesitancy in accosting camera-laden strangers thus:

"Would you like a really choice shot for your album? I'm former national cornhusking champion of the world. I'll be glad to pose for you."

Sometimes he finds a sucker who's too timid to refuse him. But mostly the amateurs and the professionals with cameras just look him over for an Allis-Chalmers or a Mc-Cormick-Deering label, and walk away shaking their heads sadly.

Cornhusking by hand is a lost art. Milking by hand is getting that way. Several generations of female dairy calves have grown up to adulthood and senility and been converted into hamburger without even feeling the touch of the human palm.

Farm populations are dropping steadily as machines do more work and men do less. But metropolitan populations are going up and up because it takes more men to build the machines that take the place of the men on the farms.

Yet the scattered farmers of western Wisconsin still decide critical elections. This is true for a very simple reason: Since the days of the American Revolution, the men of the soil have been more fiercely jealous of their political rights than the men at the industrial machines. A farmer will wallow through nine miles of mud to cast his angry vote while a sprinkle keeps his city brother home from the polls

two blocks away. Industrial workers are becoming more
and more conscious of their political obligations, but it's
a slow and laborious improvement.

That's why the farm revolt against mccarthyism in Wisconsin is so significant. The farmers elected Joe by a fairly
narrow margin. The farmers could and would recall him if
they had the chance.

While the Wisconsin "hayseeds" readily concede the
growing importance of industry, we recognize that this
industrial economy is built upon a strong and prosperous
agriculture. Without dairy cows, the thump of the heavy
metal presses would be silenced in Racine, West Allis, and
Kenosha, and Milwaukee beer would turn flat in the kegs
for lack of customers.

The trouble with the leadership of both major parties
in Wisconsin is that they don't consult the Guy on the
Back Forty, and the Guy on the Back Forty is getting
pretty fed up with them.

He isn't a man to go in for fancy stuff like moral principles in politics. More often than not he's inclined to the
cynical belief that all politicians are crooks. He's been sold
down the river so often that maybe he has a point.

The average Wisconsin farmer is a Republican by habit,
but he will kick over the party traces a lot quicker than
his city brother. He recognizes the merit of organization,
but he's so widely scattered and so intensely jealous of his
individual rights that he doesn't know quite how to go
about it.

Get almost any ten farmers together and you've got at
least three different ideas of what should be done to solve

the farm crisis. Get twenty farmers together and you've probably got three new farm organizations, all of them so busily engaged fighting each other that they have little time or energy to engage their common strength against a common enemy.

Politically, in times of economic stress, the attitude of the Wisconsin dairy farmer is best illustrated by a grim and grizzled old Norwegian I met going into the polling place.

"Who are you going to vote for, Ole?" I inquired.

"I didn't come to vote fer," Ole snorted. "I come to vote against."

Ole has suddenly and definitely decided to strike Joe out the next time Joe comes up to bat. Ole's reasons are simple and understandable. So long as the prices of eggs and milk were high enough so Ole could afford a new car every couple of years, pay his taxes, and send the kids to school, he was satisfied. Joe's antics were kind of amusing, and the Guy on the Back Forty can use a good laugh now and then. But these days the price of eggs and milk isn't so good.

"What," Ole is asking, "has Joe ever done for me?"

Few Wisconsin farmers have ever seen a Communist. Joe's Commie search is purely academic, so far as Ole is concerned. The price of milk isn't academic. Ole is beginning to scrutinize Joe's farm record. It's a record of voting against, or failing to vote for, most farm legislation. It's getting tougher and tougher to hide that record behind an army of Communists Joe didn't catch.

The Revolt Against McCarthy is no less evident in the

small rural towns and the rural cities of Wisconsin. I visited dozens of them during the first recall effort, and this is how it went:

Sheboygan

Here I found what was probably Wisconsin's best-organized recall group. From publicity to the canvass for signers the job was done with skilled precision.

The public meeting was attended by a heartening assortment of workers, business and professional men. The show was stolen by Fred Clark, an irresistible Irishman who bobbed up with an unscholarly but understandable explanation of Joe McCarthy.

"Us Irish are fine people," he boasted, reasonably enough, "but there are those among us who have a passion for the spotlight. If I sat through this meeting without all of you looking at me at least once, I'd probably run a temperature of 104. Joe's that way. Anything to keep people looking his way. Right now Joe's gag is Communism. But if the people start yawning at the Communism gag, Joe will come up with another."

Green Bay

This is a town where you don't dare utter an unkind word about the Packers or Joe McCarthy unless you're alone on the premises or wearing a suit of armor.

The recall meeting was scheduled in the supervisor's room at the county courthouse. All day the county clerk had been given a rough time by the pro-McCarthy fanatics because he had granted permission to the recall committee to hold its meeting there. But, even though I heard he was of the pro-McCarthy persuasion, he stuck by his guns. He believed that the Constitution meant what it said when it guaranteed freedom of assembly and freedom of speech. Public officials in other Wisconsin towns, where the recall movement was denied access to public meeting places, apparently hadn't read the Constitution.

Quite a few Green Bay citizens were all for repealing this portion of the Constitution by violence. Two dozen of them stood out in the corridor. Once when I passed by one of the group called out: "How'd you like to be tarred and feathered and rode out of town on a rail?"

"That kind of publicity might be worth some personal discomfort," I conceded. "It would show the country what mccarthyism does to apparently sane and normal citizens."

After that the crowd contented itself with standing in the hallway and shouting noisily: "Door for Gore" and "Joe Must Stay."

Inside, there was quite a crowd of attentive Green Bay citizens. They strongly favored giving Joe the boot, but none of them had the urge to serve as chairman. They feared what might happen to their businesses and their reputations. Ultimately, Bob Houle volunteered.

Bob Houle is a tall, well-proportioned young Irish Catholic with a highly developed sense of moral obligation. He's long been a personable and popular radio newsman and television personality in the Green Bay area. He was, in fact, a friendly acquaintance of Joe McCarthy until Joe appeared on his radio program back in 1952. Joe was going through his usual act.

"I am now showing Bob Houle documented evidence of what I am telling you," he would say.

"He had no such evidence," Bob told us. "All he had in his hand was a sheet of blank paper. I've been an honest reporter in Green Bay too long to stand for that kind of nonsense on my program. I said so. Joe and I haven't been friends since."

Houle, a young and far from wealthy married man with a family, made a mighty sacrifice with that chairmanship decision. Furthermore, he knew he was making a sacrifice. Next night in a spectacular broadcast he was the leading news item on the WBAY-TV news program. He resigned from his two television shows to spare his sponsors embarrassment.

"We'll eat somehow," Houle said grimly. "A guy's got to live with his conscience."

The world could use a lot more Bob Houles.

Five members of the Green Bay *Press-Gazette* staff attended the meeting. I liked them, and I hope they liked me. But the *P-G* news policy and the news policy of the Appleton *Post-Crescent*, its full sister, has always reminded me of a music editor I once knew who always made his reporters wear earplugs when they covered a Wagner concert because he didn't like Wagner. For me this was not a new conception of *P-G* news policy. This policy first became apparent to me when I was editing the Clintonville newspaper not too many miles from either of these pleasant cities.

It is not unusual for newspapers to suspect those who disagree with them of stupidity. I've been guilty of that fantasy, even when my own enlightenment has been fairly recent. The Green Bay and Appleton newspapers carry it a step further. Those who disagree with them are not only stupid people, they must, perforce, be bad people.

They have built a strange world populated by unworldly caricatures. In this world there are only heroes and heroines among the people who believe with them, and villains and villainesses among the people who disagree. There are no half-heroes, no half-villains.

The folks who yearned to tar and feather me weren't bad people. Not even naughty people. A little on the prankish side, maybe. *We* were the bad people for starting a recall which got them into that prankish state of mind. In *our* weakest moments *we* sometimes wish wistfully that we possessed this brand of smug, virtuous complacency. There's never any doubt in the editorial den of the *Press-Gazette* who's going to get into heaven—the folks who vote for Joseph Raymond McCarthy and a straight Republican ticket.

On September 1, 1954, Bob Houle moved his family to California.

"If I thought the next recall effort needed me, I'd stay here if I had to dig ditches," he said. "But with the kind of organization job you're doing, it can't miss. You'll get plenty of help from Green Bay and Brown County. There has been an amazing and extensive switch in sentiment. If I had it to do over, I'd do the same thing again, even though I knew I would have to leave my home town.

Our roots are deep here, but there is no future for me here under present conditions. You may be sure that I shall continue to fight for freedom and for honesty in politics wherever I go."

Appleton

The most amazing experience of a most amazing seventy days was unquestionably our experience in Joe's "adopted home town." We'd already hit an unexpected bonanza of petition signatures from Appleton, but we'd had a sufficient number of nasty, anonymous letters from the same source to prompt us to expect practically anything after our Green Bay experience. Nothing like that happened for an obvious reason. The pro-McCarthy folks didn't know where we were meeting. Neither, unhappily, did some of the anti-McCarthy folks.

My first hint that we were due for an unusual experience came over my car radio as I approached Appleton. I was listening to a local radio broadcast.

"The Appleton Joe Must Go Club is meeting here tonight, but no one knows where."

At the local hotel we were joined by Harold Michael, state president of the recall. Presently Bill Mitchell called for us. Bill is only one of the recall workers who made Appleton such an unexpectedly pleasant spot for us. I omit the names of others, not for lack of appreciation, but in the fear that identification might hurt them. The pro-McCarthy forces of Green Bay, Appleton, and Oshkosh are probably the most violent in the state. Mitchell, an industrial engineer with a solid reputation, is apparently untouchable.

Never since the old days when a guy went down a flight of dark stairs, knocked three times, and asked for Charlie to get a ten-cent mug of beer for half a rock have I had an experience like this. We met in the comfortable, isolated basement of a manufacturing plant. The room was jammed to overflowing. Professors and students rubbed elbows with executives and guys from the production line. It was an encouraging meeting. Men and women came up afterward, shook my hand, and said: "We first began to doubt Joe when he attacked Dr. Pusey. We've had plenty of reason to doubt him since. We'll do what we can."

A sincere young lady was there from the Appleton *Post-Crescent* which, like its sister at Green Bay, passionately believes in democracy for those who believe as the *P-C* believes. The young lady was a little jumpy, and almost as confused as I was. When I saw her story next day I understood. She was bewildered no end to discover that I was respectably dressed, and if I had horns they didn't show.

Madison

There probably isn't another city in the whole world like Madison, Wisconsin. . . . Madison, where a great university lauds the virtues of higher education, and points with pride to "The Old Grass Cutter" Roundy Coughlin, who has carved a fortune out of bad grammar . . . Mad-

ison, where two newspapers under the same ownership
scream insults at each other in their daily newspaper columns. . . . Madison, where people have a childish faith
that two hundred-pound all-America halfbacks enroll at
the University of Wisconsin because they like the view of
Lake Minona, but nobody trusts the governor's income tax
statement.

Quite a few pleasant people turned out for our meeting
at Turner Hall. They applauded my usual inept speech
charitably. The older generation came up to shake hands
and beam at me. The youngsters did the work.

I don't know whether Madison loves me or not, but I
love Madison. Maybe Madison has more frailties than
most cities, but it also has a larger assortment of virtues.
Its traffic rules defy human logic, but they're the essence
of simplicity and common sense compared with Madison
politics, in which stern virtue is mixed generously with
the morality of an Al Capone mobster. Madison makes
about as much sense as a three hundred-pound television
wrestler with cauliflower ears crocheting a three-inch
lace doily.

But I love it!

The Madison-Dane County recall group did a thorough
and intelligent job. They used radio, television, and the
newspapers to supplement an effective, hard-working
organization. They encountered two annoying road
blocks.

Madison has a long history of "choosing up sides" on
any political issue. The foxy pro-McCarthy forces circulated a story that the recall was a "left-wing movement."

The attempt was to lose the issue of mccarthyism in a heavy fog of personal prejudice, and the attempt was fairly successful. This type of political personality will almost certainly insist on looking through the latest census records of Saint Peter before they pass through the pearly gates.

The second strategy was the strategy of fear. Not altogether the fear of retaliation against those who signed or circulated. Lots of well-tagged anti-McCarthy folks refused to work or sign merely because of the fear of failure. They'd been persuaded that the recall couldn't work. They didn't want to be identified with a lost cause. The fear of failure has defeated more worthy causes than the obstacles in the path of success. If the fear of failure had worked on Columbus and George Washington, America would never have been discovered and the American Revolution would never have been fought.

One news commentator chronically referred to the recall workers as the Bumblebees. Any engineer can prove that it's impossible for the bumblebee to fly. He hasn't sufficient wing span to carry his weight. But the bumblebee, too stupid to know all this, goes ahead and flies anyway.

Madison was also the scene of the daffiest TV show in which I've ever participated. I still wake up at night in a cold sweat dreaming about it. It was one of those round-table affairs in which Morrie Rubin, editor of the *Progressive* magazine, and I matched wits, if it may be called that, with Mrs. Grace Livesy and a young fellow from Milwaukee. Mrs. Livesy is president of the Wisconsin chapter of the For America party. The young man was also for America—and Joe McCarthy.

Mrs. Livesy is easy enough to look at. Furthermore, she knows her TV audiences. Oscar Rennebohn's drugstore must have done a right smart piece of business with her that afternoon. It was distributed in the right places, too.

Early in my brief and unspectacular television career someone instructed me: "Wear a blue suit and a blue tie. Don't waste time cultivating the president of the television station. Get in solid with the sound man who controls the boom mike."

McCarthy's apostles are uniformly skilled in Joe's technique of grabbing a mike and running away with it in a forum discussion like Bronco Nagurski running away with a football. Mrs. Livesy, take it from one who knows, is no exception.

Like Joe, his disciples don't like to confuse the issue with facts. Morrie and I asked them, since Joe was such a great Communist chaser, to name in a hurry three Communists he'd caught. As I recall it, they gave us names of three guys who either had never been convicted, or were convicted years before Joe started chasing Commies. They also dusted off the well-worn gag about Joe being the only logical savior of mankind. You had a feeling that if Joe should drop over dead, we might just as well sail back in the *Mayflower* and give the country back to the Indians. If one kind of Reds didn't take it over, another would.

Mrs. Livesy, who seemed to be a reasonable lady on

such subjects as the weather and the evils of dandelions in the front lawn, was still talking three minutes after the forum ended and the mikes were shut off.

Thirteen telephone calls were registered at the switchboard before we hustled out of the studio. Eleven of them wanted Mrs. Livesy kept off the air. One wanted me thrown bodily out of the studio. The thirteenth guy, obviously a hopeless neurotic, said he was selling his television set and using the proceeds to finance an Association to Encourage Deafness in the United States.

Milwaukee

Milwaukee is "Wisconsin's biggest small town." It's full of beer, baseball, wienerschnitzels, and "No Parking" signs.

It is also full of people who have been nauseated by mccarthyism much longer and much more violently than I have. The trouble is, they've been hating mccarthyism too long—so long that they're resigned to mccarthyism, and thoroughly convinced that nobody can do anything about it.

They're like the man with the chronic pain in the neck. The doctor keeps giving him pills, and putting him through expensive and extensive courses of light treatments. The pain persists. The patient finally gives up even believing he can be cured. By this time he's so used to the pain in the neck he'd feel kind of lonesome without it.

Lots of people did get excited about the recall in Milwaukee, but lots of people didn't. The Milwaukee *Journal* didn't, although the *Journal* is a weary, punch-drunk, and long-time sparring partner of McCarthy. We had a frustrated feeling at times that the *Journal* wasn't even listening to us through its cauliflower ears, and wasn't seeing us through its blackened and bloodshot eyes. A slightly bitter reporter ventured the opinion that the *Journal* and the *Cap-Times* were slow in joining us because "they think they have a patent for fighting McCarthy in Wisconsin, and you're infringing on their patent."

This wasn't strictly true. The *Journal* and *Cap-Times* had seen a lot of hairy-chested giants come out confidently to do battle with mccarthyism. They'd seen Joe follow the advice of the now-famous Indian named Charlie to "kick 'em in the crotch, and kick 'em first." Too often they'd seen Joe leering triumphantly as the hairy-chested giants were carried out of the ring on a stretcher.

They frequently hailed the moral virtue of the recall movement in stirring language. But they weren't going to be trapped again into chanting "Hail the new champ!" and eating their words shortly thereafter. Obviously, this anaemic, spindle-legged, sunken-chested challenger wouldn't last more than a round against Joe's bulging muscles of deceit and slander.

The labor unions at the top level had the same attitude for the same reason, plus an additional ingredient—the ingredient of fear.

This fear sprang from three sources. The unions had a ticklish and important legislative battle ahead of them. They knew too well how effectively and how brutally

Joseph Raymond McCarthy could strike at them through an unfortunate public prejudice against unions. The CIO particularly made no secret of an unhappy Communist history back in the middle forties. These were the same Commies who helped elect Joseph Raymond McCarthy in 1946. The CIO had unquestionably put its house in order. Joseph Raymond says he'd put his house in order. But you may be sure he wouldn't hesitate to point a finger of accusation at the CIO for a 1946 blunder to which he was a gleeful partner.

There were two other fears. There was a sincere fear that open union participation would injure the recall. There was the fear that heavy financial demands would be made upon the union treasury when union funds were needed for other purposes.

I am not one to berate the unions or the Democratic party for failing to identify themselves with the recall officially for what they believed to be good and sufficient reasons. Thousands of hard-working Democrats and union members did identify themselves with the recall. Their efforts were indispensable.

For many years I have been a Republican and a resident of rural areas where large labor organizations do not exist. If the recall has accomplished nothing else, it has taught me and a great many other rural Republicans that the labor bosses and the Democrats are not the unsavory characters we may have assumed them to be. Labor unions are competently guided by men of breadth and vision. The honest and able Democrats are found in about the same proportion as honest and able Republicans. I doubt if this realization has made me a worse Republican. I'm sure it has made me a better American.

I would like to pay personal tribute to the thousands of little people whose faith and industry I have so much appreciated. But I cannot for lack of space, and for fear that identification may harm them. I choose only a few Milwaukeeans whose efforts on behalf of the recall are so well known that their names can scarcely escape public notice.

There is Senator Henry Maier, for instance. Henry is the man who almost singlehandedly won the fight for a reapportionment of Wisconsin's assembly and senatorial districts on a population basis. He invented that dastardly name "areacrat," and used it effectively against us country bumpkins who preferred reapportionment on a basis of population and area. He conceived the famous "Paul Revere's Ride," which broke into *Life* magazine when Paul's horse tumbled on Wisconsin Avenue. He whaled the daylights out of us, and we should hate him, but we don't. Henry has won a lot of fights, but he's never won one by "kicking the other guy in the crotch, and kicking him first."

Henry would like to have you believe he's very tough and completely practical. He's a phony. His heart is as big as a house, and his conscience speaks to him with considerable authority. That's why Henry is such a power in his district and in the state senate. You may not agree with him, but it's difficult to deny that Senator Maier is an honest man. Money and power won't sway him. If they would, Senator Maier could have lots more of both.

I remember how Henry used to come over to our meetings, pound the table, and shout in a loud, pleasant voice: "I wouldn't touch this recall with a ten-foot pole. It's run by a bunch of amateurs who don't know which end is up. It's a laugh. Henry Maier is a practical man."

But he kept coming to the meetings. He pounded the table with less and less vigor. One day he didn't pound the table at all.

"Listen, you jerks," he said. "There's only one way you can make this thing work——"

After that Henry Maier—the tough, practical guy who wouldn't touch an amateur movement with a ten-foot pole—was with us all the way.

Republican Senator Harry Franke is cut from the same piece of cloth, although the two men are miles apart politically and in their manner of approach. Franke is smooth, soft-spoken, and the senatorial representative from Milwaukee's "silk-stocking" district where McCarthy is reputed to have his strongest support. It took a great deal of courage for Franke, a man on the brink of a great political career, to step out of the McCarthy parade. It would have been easy for Franke to have said: "I'll help you quietly, but don't identify me publicly with this thing."

Don't tell me that honest politicians are a vanished race. So long as there are Senator Frankes and Senator Maiers you and I may face the future with considerable confidence. The Frankes and the Maiers obviously cannot always be right, since they frequently disagree, but men of integrity ultimately come up with the right answer out of their disagreement. Dishonest men invariably come up with the wrong answer, even when they agree.

I'll say as much for Casimir Kendziorski, a native of Poland and the big political wheel in Milwaukee's famed Polish district. I was not too surprised when a Poles for McCarthy Club announced its intention of blocking the recall. I had, in fact, assumed that the Poles might be pro-McCarthy for reasons which I could understand. The Poles, more than any other people, have suffered terrible injustices at the hands of the Communists. Wouldn't it be natural for them to swallow the fallacy that they must support McCarthy to be anti-Communist?

Kendziorski, a peppery little man with the tongue of a serpent when his moral virtue is assaulted, said "No" in stirring terms. Speaking of the Poles for McCarthy Club he declared:

"Three Poles they were, three Poles they are, three Poles apart they will be. My people are not gullible. They see mccarthyism for what it is—a phony and a danger no less acute than Communism."

The Poles for McCarthy Club died aborning. One night out in a precinct where the good people of Polish ancestry are thicker than shamrock in Dublin on St. Patrick's Day I watched one of the exciting Milwaukee mass mobilizations. I've never seen so many consonants on so many sheets of paper in all my life. I came away with a warm and comforting feeling for the people of Polish descent.

In Milwaukee, too, I arrived at a new appreciation for the courage of racial groups. Watching a south-side mobilization in a rainstorm, I found shelter under a convenient awning. I was approached in late afternoon by a husky Negro of perhaps thirty years, a packing-house employee.

"We want to sign, but some of us are afraid," he told me. We've been told that we will lose our jobs, or our homes. If you would speak to us, Mr. Gore, it might help."

We found two dozen of them in a nearby restaurant. In the back room I listened with sympathy to their problem. The minority peoples are the first to bear the strongest and cruelest blows of hysteria.

"I would not blame you for refusing to sign," I conceded, "even though I doubt if any harm will come to you. But remember this: If you fail to sign now, the day may come when the right to sign will be denied you. If you do sign, I promise that no one will see your name, if the recall fails."

I made that promise many times to many people in the days ahead. I want to make that perfectly clear because some weeks afterward I was accused of indulging in "melodrama" because I refused to deliver those petitions upon the order of the district attorney in my county.

Every Negro in that dingy back room signed the recall petition. I have never been prouder of any group of American citizens than I was of those Negroes who fought with their fears, and won the battle. Many thousands of my own race were not so brave. In the words of Senator Franke:

"They fear that if they sign, a big prison truck may drive up to their door, and they may be spirited away to a concentration camp."

Three active and well-organized Milwaukee groups worked on the recall until the bitter end: The Citizens Against McCarthy, sponsored by the labor groups; the Joe Must Go Club of Milwaukee, sponsored by faithful Democrats and faithful Republicans working in remarkable harmony; and the Mothers' March on McCarthy.

Numerically, the latter organization was the least important, but it was undeniably interesting. Angie Vail, wife of Milwaukee advertising executive Robert K. Vail, organized mothers and housewives with vim and vigor. Most of the gals didn't know a Republican from a Democrat without a score card, but they knew that the example of Senator McCarthy was a bad example for their children.

They not only financed all their activities, but they contributed to the state movement by a simple device which would probably never occur to a man. They bought petitions from their club for five cents each, then they went from house to house and filled the petitions with names.

It was a delightful organization. One night Angie sat in on a state steering committee meeting. At one point there was considerable wrangling over procedures.

"We never have this trouble," Angie confided to me in a loud voice. "We never have any meetings."

On Mother's Day the Mothers March sent a beautiful bouquet of red roses to my wife with this brief message: "For the hardships you have endured without complaint and without headlines."

That was the night a rock came sailing through the window of our living room. The rock didn't make my wife cry, but the roses did.

Most spectacular of the Milwaukee recall devices was the fleet of ten sound trucks that visited the factory gates. In the morning the men manning the trucks passed out empty petitions; in the evening they collected the filled petitions and notarized them. The same trucks did a thriving business at the county stadium, "Home of the Braves." Gallup has never taken a separate poll of sports fans, but we had a hunch it might reveal a remarkably high anti-McCarthy sentiment. Sportsmen have a greater sense of fair play than non-sportsmen.

Less spectacular was the effective street-corner campaign during busy shopping periods. The men and women circulators were spit at, they were called unbelievably filthy names, they were threatened with physical violence, their cars were damaged, but they kept at the job with grim courage.

There were some experiences not quite so pleasant. Even though I spent the three convention days in the Schroeder Hotel, I missed all sessions of the Wisconsin Press Association for the first time in fourteen years. A resolution by the pro-McCarthy editors to oust me never got presented. But there were symptoms that such a resolution might be introduced if I appeared. I balked at the prospect of turning the WPA convention into a recall debate, in which harmony might be destroyed for years to come, and in which nothing constructive would be accomplished either for the press of the state or the recall movement. Secretary Carl Zielke's ulcers are bad enough in a situation of comparative calm. Being a kind and gentle soul, I have no desire to launch an epidemic of ulcers.

Friday noon McCarthy was addressing the Wisconsin Press Women. Some of the boys figured it might be good politics for me to greet him as he exited from the hotel. I took a front seat in the coffee-shop with a dozen of my acquaintances. But when Joe made his exit, he was surrounded by what his severest critics often describe as "The Twenty Goons." They look neither to the right nor the left. Neither does Joseph Raymond. In fact, they outsped Joe's recently acquired wife Jean, who was still hobbling along on crutches sixteen paces back. After only a few weeks of marriage it seemed to us that sixteen paces were too many paces to separate a devoted husband from his ailing wife, but every man and woman to his or her taste.

There were other symptoms that Joe and his boys had no intention of getting caught in the same precinct with the recall.

A radio newscaster called me excitedly one afternoon at Milwaukee with a real charming idea. Joe was to arrive by plane at the airport near Fort Atkinson, my old home town, where Joe was to deliver a major address that evening. His scheduled arrival time was five-thirty. Wouldn't it be a good gag to meet Joe at the airport? Corny, maybe, but interesting. Joe got in two hours ahead of schedule.

Irv Cherdron, one of the tireless workers for the recall, in fact a guy who toyed with the idea of a Joe Must Go movement long before it occurred to me, telephoned me from Marshfield, Wisconsin, one night when I was in Buffalo. Joe was to make a speech at a dairy picnic at nearby Athens the following day. Irv contended that the Sauk-Prairie *Star,* as the state's leading weekly dairy news-paper, should have a proper place on the program. He was talking at the time with one of Joe's local managers.

"Gore can have twenty minutes," the man said.

Next morning I called back to make sure the man wasn't speaking out of too many beers. He squirmed a little. Sure, he and Joe would be glad to relinquish a por-tion of Joe's time, but arrangements were in the hands of the committee, a complication he hadn't mentioned when he was boasting before witnesses the night before.

Cherdron chased the committee madly over the county. He found the members huddled in the office of the Mosi-nee *Times,* from which Francis Schweinler had blown a mighty bugle for Joe during the last campaign. You guessed it. The program was full to overflowing.

There was a national forum radio program on which I was scheduled with Roy Cohn. At the last moment Jenkins and Mundt decided it would be inadvisable for Cohn to discuss issues over the air while the hearings were in progress.

Senator McCarthy and Roy Cohn weren't afraid of me. Likely they'd have torn me to bleeding shreds. But when Joe disclaimed all knowledge of the recall he was indulging in the same kind of unrealistic thinking as the loyal Wisconsin citizen who sits out on the lake shore telling the tourist from Kansas that there are no mos-quitoes in Wisconsin and scratching like mad.

In Milwaukee there was just one sour note during all my visits. One of the Milwaukee hotels had plenty of rooms until they discovered I was to be their guest, when the supply of rooms suddenly vanished. We tried it a second time by telephone just to make sure.

Milwaukee, I cheerfully concede, isn't 100 per cent anti-McCarthy—yet. But I understand that Milwaukee isn't 100 per cent beer and baseball, either.

DOWN THE

HOME STRETCH . . .

Never have I admitted publicly how badly things were going with the recall until those closing weeks. We knew we had a lot of signatures. But where were they? They weren't in our office.

Bob Stevens finished his testimony in the Army-McCarthy Big Fuss. It wasn't good. I heard people say on the streets, in planes, trains, restaurants:

"Maybe McCarthy's bad, but the Army's bad, too."

I was furious, but there wasn't much I could do about it. Obviously Stevens, an able and wealthy executive, had been a frequent associate of the prominent Cohn and Schine families. There's nothing unusual or startling about

that. Obviously, he'd tried to play patty-cake with Joe Mc-
Carthy, and obviously Joe had slugged him in the solar
plexus. Why didn't he say so?

The apparent answer was that he couldn't say so. It was
one of those things a guy couldn't explain, but why didn't
the radio-television audience see it?

Sure, there was the fake photo, the partially phony letter, typical of the McCarthy technique. But folks shrugged
them off. After all, a photo *was* taken with Stevens and
Schine on it. A letter *was* written by the FBI. Adams
started out good, but he got his conversational feet all
tangled up under persistent questioning. Those were dark
days indeed.

Funny thing about a TV screen. You take a quick look,
you see the quick, superficial things. But after weeks and
weeks a man's soul begins to show up on his face. The soul
of mccarthyism began to show, and it wasn't a pretty soul.

Joe helped by overplaying his hand. Joe's never been
as bright politically as he's reputed to be by his friends
and his enemies. He just grabbed a good, sound act and
kept repeating it, like the life of the party who knows one
funny story and keeps telling it over and over. Along about
midnight it gets pretty tiresome, even if the guests are
somewhat diluted with martinis.

Joe kept grabbing the mike and holding it. This was effective for a while, but the American public is essentially
fair minded. Pretty soon Gus Klambaker out in the hills
got to figuring: "This guy McCarthy is beefing because
the Army's holding up the works with these silly hearings,
but he's doing most of the talking. Maybe he is a phony."

Joe may well have committed political suicide with the Freddy Fisher incident. A lot of American stomachs turned that morning, and most of them never turned back. Even Joe's press corps broke ranks. The *State Journal* at Madison, which had never before doused Joe with anything less than expensive cologne, found his performance revolting. Even the Chicago *Tribune* closed its eyes and shuddered briefly.

Out in Sauk City we knew the score in a hurry. One morning it took two mailbags to bring in the petitions to the recall headquarters. Joe Must Go Clubs all over the state began reporting news of the avalanche.

In my Milwaukee hotel room I did some long and careful figuring. I telephoned Ben Leighton at the Sauk City recall office to verify my figures. I've never met many statisticians, but if they're all like Ben Leighton, I have a profound respect for their trade.

Ben knows Wisconsin as he knows the floor plan of his Baraboo home. He'd sorted the rural communities from the city communities and the small towns from the big towns; he'd sorted the slow-moving and the fast-moving communities; he'd sorted the rock-ribbed and the vacillating communities. A week before it happened, he'd predicted that Joe's following was tottering as a result of the hearings, and we were about to be buried in petitions. He knew where the names were coming from, and when they would arrive. More than that, I don't know much about his methods, but I know they work. I have often suspected that he is in league with a friendly tribe of witches.

We had something over 300,000 signatures on hand,

most of which hadn't been sorted for technical errors. They were arriving at Sauk City and the dozens of collecting centers faster than the crews could take care of them.

A few weeks before I would have been happy about a protest of 125,000 names. Now I was unhappy because we would probably fall slightly short of 403,804.

"Maybe a miracle will happen," I suggested.

"A miracle has already happened," Ben reminded me. "It isn't that the signers aren't there. But you've got to remember these 6,500 circulators are volunteer workers. It's physically impossible for them to gather that many names in the time that's left."

"There must be *something* we can do," I persisted. "When we're this close——"

There was a long, long pause. Statisticians are presumed to be emotionless robots, but I detected a sob in Ben's voice.

"Listen, *I'm* just as anxious as you that this effort succeed. I'd be delighted to be proved a liar. Sure, it could work. Joe could strangle Welch in front of the television cameras with 40,000,000 people watching, and maybe a miracle would happen in Wisconsin. But my best guess is that we will wind up 50,000 short of our goal."

There was another long pause.

"It's a magnificent effort," Ben said. "There's never been anything like it in the history of the country."

"No," I said. "I guess not."

Neither of us felt much like talking. We hung up.

A statewide "final report" over a state-wide radio hookup was scheduled for Thursday night. For two days it had been raining most of the time in Milwaukee. Late that aft-

ernoon I was out in the rain visiting with circulators and
signers. I had less than two hours to get to Madison,
eighty-four hours away, when I stepped on the starter of
my car at the parking lot. Nothing happened. I tried again
and again. So did the parking-lot attendant. The rain was
so blinding by this time I couldn't see across the street.
The motor was drenched. So was I. And in ninety minutes
I was due for a state-wide broadcast almost ninety miles
away.

Reid Ross, a Milwaukee member of our steering committee, knew the boys at the Milwaukee station on
the chain. They were mighty nice about it. They didn't
know what could be done, but they'd try. I don't know
much about radios except how to turn them on, but it
seems every transformer or something along the line had
to be turned around if the broadcast was to go on from
Milwaukee instead of Madison. For a few minutes I feared
they'd have to bring Alexander Graham Bell back to life.

At three minutes before broadcast time word came from
the telephone corporation: "We're on."

It was a large, pleasant room there in Milwaukee with
a clock on the far wall, me and the microphones in the
middle. I began to talk. I kept thinking about those 6,500
circulators out there in that driving rain working hopeful-
ly for a goal they couldn't reach. Time would run out on
them.

My eyes blurred so I couldn't see my script. I kept talking. Faces kept bobbing up in front of me—the faces of
people who had made real long sacrifices because they
believed this was a moral crusade.

I kept thinking of the twenty-member "steering committee" and the men and women who had come from great distances every week without reward or hope of reward . . . I kept thinking of Dick Allen out at Superior, "the faithful" at Eau Claire, Green Bay and Appleton, Janesville, Beloit, and hundreds of other towns large and small over the broad map of Wisconsin . . . . I kept thinking of John and Doris Gasser, Jack and Tom Bauer, Mrs. Loveridge and Mrs. Marquardt, and a dozen others who labored every night and many days in the state recall headquarters . . .

I kept choking up. I tried to be cheerful about the whole thing. We had a "grim, fighting chance," I said. But when I had finished and sat staring at that chromium mike, the mike leered at me.

The girl at the switchboard asked me to take a call. It was one of the Milwaukee circulators.

"You were wonderful," she said, and I could tell she was choking up a little, too. "Don't be afraid of losing. We can't lose. We've won already, and we'll do the job we've set out to do next time if we don't do it this time."

Chet Roberts, who had worked diligently on the recall with an effective knowledge gained from many years in the Republican vineyards, called to say the same thing.

I walked out into the rain with Reid Ross, wondering how many hearts I had broken in Wisconsin during those twelve minutes.

The rest is history.

The recall effort was to end officially the following Saturday. Friday I drive to Menominee, Wisconsin, with my family to watch my youngest son graduate from Stout

Institute. That night we drove to Spring Valley, where I had spent almost five pleasant years editing the *Sun*. Spring Valley is a brave and charming village nestled in the wooded foothills of the scenic Eau Galle River. It is full of Norwegians and Republicans. It had also been full of vigorous pro-McCarthyites. I wondered if the people still felt the same way. This was my first trip back in two years.

That night I took a petition downtown to one of the stores. I laid it on the counter and greeted my friends. In less than an hour sixteen shoppers, mostly from the nearby town of Gilman, had signed. Eleven of them volunteered the information that they had voted for McCarthy in November 1952.

All the following week signatures kept pouring into the recall offices. Signers knew they were too late for legality, but they had a burning desire to demonstrate a strong and sudden protest against mccarthyism.

The final signature count was sufficient for a recall. But some 70,000 signatures were invalidated for various reasons—some were before or after the sixty-day time limit, some petitions weren't notarized, some had signers from two counties on the same petition. The legal signatures exceeded a third of a million—a sufficient number to force McCarthy into a recall following any election except the record election of 1952.

We had sent cards to circulators asking for a record of signatures which hadn't been sent to any recall headquarters for one reason or another. They totaled 30,000.

Ben Leighton is a disgustingly accurate man sometimes.

THE ELEPHANT

LABORED AND BEGAT

AN ANT...

With the close of the first recall effort, I welcomed the prospect of returning to my calm and modest labors at the helm of a small country weekly. I envisioned getting acquainted with my family again, catching up with my golf and my fishing. I am still, somewhat wistfully, contemplating that prospect in the somewhat remote future.

Strangely, the first recall effort became bigger news after it had ended in failure than it ever was during those frenzied days when it had a chance of success.

Three men were largely responsible—Harlan Kelley, district attorney for Sauk County; Roman Reuter, the self-confessed 200-per-cent American who launched the Door

for Gore Club; and Darrel McIntyre, the self-appointed re-
incarnation of Clarence Darrow. There were other minor
characters involved in the wings and in front of footlights,
but they will make their appearance as the narrative pro-
gresses.

The initial complication of this bizarre plot presented
itself at the most critical stage of the recall effort. Anti-
McCarthy sentiment was visibly and audibly mounting
in the state. Eisenhower Republicans, suddenly and painfully aware that the President and the Administration were
among the major targets of McCarthy, were openly revolting. Democrats were beginning to recognize that mccarthyism was more than a convenient Ism at which they
could point a finger of derision; it was a alarming nationalistic menace to the future and the freedoms of the nation.
Mothers were saying: "That man is rude and insufferable."

It was evident that the recall headquarters was being
suddenly smothered in an avalanche of petitions. I made
a national appeal via press, radio, and television for $15,-
000 to finance a state-wide "family-size" petition and a
tabloid newspaper exposé of the sad McCarthy record.

At this critical moment we were shocked to read in our
daily newspapers and hear over the radio one morning
that Harlan Kelley, district attorney for my home county
and presumably my friend, suspected "grave symptoms of
political corruption" in Sauk County. The same spectacular news release indicated that Kelley would call up for
questioning before a Baraboo justice of the peace Joe Must
Go Treasurer Carl Lachmund and Executive Secretary
Leroy Gore.

Under Wisconsin law, John Doe inquiries are of two varieties. There is a provision for a secret inquiry, in which the principals and the nature of the inquiry are kept from the public. This procedure is logically used for the public protection in investigations of violations where secrecy aids and abets justice. An open hearing is customarily called to investigate public affairs where public records are involved.

In a secret investigation the witnesses may be denied counsel and a transcript of the testimony. In neither case are the witnesses accused of a crime. They are merely called upon to testify so a court may determine whether or not a crime has been committed.

Not until forty-eight hours after I read in the press and heard from the airways that I was to be called before a "secret inquiry" were subpoenas served upon me. This procedure was frequently repeated during the extended course of the "inquiry." Headlines, in which the district attorney's "suspicions" were used to discredit us personally and as an organization, were invariably much more spectacular than the "inquiry" that followed them. Obviously the district attorney's unusual method of keeping a secret was to tell 1,500 newspapers, several thousand broadcasters, and all available press services.

Simultaneously, Attorney Darrel McIntyre filed a petition with the county judge, on behalf of his clients Roman Reuter and the Door for Gore Club, seeking the appointment of Attorney McIntyre as special counsel to investigate the Joe Must Go Club. McIntyre was equipped with a strange set of qualifications to investigate any kind of "corruption." I quote from the Chicago *Sun-Times,* Tuesday, July 13, 1954:

"The mink rancher then enlisted the legal aid of Darrel McIntyre, a criminal lawyer in Madison who has a summer place near Reuter's minks.

"McIntyre has had a colorful career. He says he is the mouthpiece for Capone hoodlums who get in trouble in Wisconsin.

"In 1941 he was suspended from the practice of law for one year by the Wisconsin Supreme Court in connection with his handling of a divorce case. He also was ordered by the court to refund an excessive fee in the probating of an estate.

" 'I'm like Clarence Darrow,' he said. 'I'll help anybody.' "

County Judge Bohn heaved the impudent McIntyre proposal out of his premises with all the vigor of a man who has picked up a lighted firecracker by mistake.

The district attorney, however, was not easily discouraged. Following a brief repetition of the "inquiry," he summoned the press to an hour-long conference which was unquestionably the wildest and most imaginative press conference in our thirty very odd years of serving up the follies of the human race in the columns of a newspaper.

The district attorney, who loves to hear himself talk and is a great hand at turning a neat phrase whether it fits the occasion or not, bluntly called us "political panhandlers" and originators of a "huge political racket."

He made the spectacular promise that the first of the following week he would serve "a large number of war-

rants against a large number of people" on such serious
criminal charges as "perjury, forgery, and obtaining
money under false pretenses."

In one violent moment of emotional absurdity he casti-
gated Ed Sachs, representing the Sauk-Prairie *Star*, and
Harold Entwhistle of the Madison *Capital-Times*.

"You are here by sufferance, not by invitation," he
shrieked. "If I were physically able, I would throw both
of you out."

Mr. Sachs, like the rest of the press, was shocked, but
not beyond words.

"Mr. Kelley," he speculated, "let us presume your investigation reveals that you have been too ambitious in
your predictions. Let us assume that you find you have no
foundation for the very serious charges you have made.
Is it then your intention to issue a denial and an apology
to clear the reputations of these people?"

"You are a very clever man, Mr. Sachs," retorted the
district attorney. "I am not a clever man. I am merely an
honest man. You are a stranger to honesty."

Sachs never got an answer to his question, but an answer really wasn't necessary, in view of Kelley's subse-
quent conduct.

Tearing a page from the manual authored by his idol,
Senator McCarthy, Kelley labeled the Sauk-Prairie *Star*
and the Madison *Capital-Times* as members of "the left-
wing press." Mr. Evjue's Madison publication is vigorous
and extremely liberal, but if it is left wing, so are most of
the people of the United States who diligently pursued
Mr. Evjue's political philosophy for two decades. As for

the Sauk-Prairie *Star*, we are slightly to the left of Colonel McCormick.

First to exit from the bizarre Kelley press conference was a lady reporter for a national magazine. She was shaking her head in stunned disbelief. "Mr. Gore," she said, "what would that man say if he really had something on somebody?"

We were unable to answer the question. I have never witnessed Mr. Kelley in action when he had anything on anybody.

But while Kelley's well-calculated antics kept us in the headlines, they inevitably hurt us far more than they helped. His threats frightened both circulators and contributors. They may well have cost us the 70,000 names we needed to win. Certainly they prevented us from collecting sufficient funds to finance a publication that might have turned defeat into victory.

As the recall effort ended, the campaign against us began to take on an unmistakable pattern. Simultaneously with our announcement that another recall effort would be made after the November elections we were attacked from several directions. Obviously, McCarthy's apostles, terrified at our near success, were determined to sabotage the next recall effort before it started.

In Milwaukee, Jack Rouse of Baraboo, executive secretary of the Republican voluntary committee of Wisconsin, demanded that the petitions be turned over for examination. He made vague threats against those who might have signed or circulated in error.

This was the tip-off that Kelley was about to subpoena

the petitions. We found no legal basis for the move. What, then, could his purpose be? Was it to prevent us from using the signatures in a future recall campaign? Was it to plague and persecute circulators and signers so they would be discouraged from taking part in the second recall effort?

There were a number of reasons why we publicly refused in advance to comply with this request.

Certainly Kelley or Rouse had no legal right to ask for the petitions. They had not been presented for legal action. They were still the property of the circulators and the recall movement.

We had publicly pledged on many occasions that we would not subject circulators and signers to public embarrassment if we failed to reach our goal.

We needed those petitions for the next recall movement, in which we propose to use those names and addresses to simplify the task of securing signatures. If they are in Kelley's possession, obviously we won't be able to use them. With his limited facilities, it would require fifty to one hundred years for Kelley to make a thorough inspection of a third of a million names. We don't want to wait that long for another recall.

We moved the bulk of the petitions to Chicago, the balance to St. Paul to avert a possible seizure action by the district attorney.

In the West Ballroom of the Conrad-Hilton Hotel, Chicago, we showed almost 300,000 names to press, radio, and television. A half dozen deep, the petitions fanned out five or six rows wide down the tables in the center of the ballroom. It was an amazing, unbelievable sight—the largest notarized petition effort in the history of the world.

Even the reporter for the strongest pro-McCarthy publication was impressed.

"I'd hate to have that many people mad at me," he confessed.

Back home, Henry Ringling of Baraboo's famed circus family, and national GOP committeeman, issued an uninspired statement that we had only 50,000 signatures. It was poorly timed, poorly planned. The press services and television cameras made it especially ridiculous.

Mr. Ringling's mistake was a not uncommon mistake; he tried to make his story too good—or too bad.

In the next breath after the 50,000 signatures monstrosity the GOP top brass, suddenly seized with an acute attack of political virtue, insisted that the petitions be brought back to Wisconsin for public inspection. The latter demand was the master stroke of County Chairman Bill Benzies, Baraboo. Even to the fairly stupid observer it was evident that the brass hats were worrying considerably more over the petition effort than 50,000 signatures would have justified.

The Kelley-Ringling-Rouse-Benzies jigsaw puzzle was complete. I put it together in a *Star* editorial this way under the following title:

"NEXT WEEK—EAST LYNNE"

"Thanks to Sauk County's busy little galaxy of McCarthy stooges, masquerading as Republican leaders, we're feeling better about the McCarthy situation every day. There must be more anti-McCarthy sentiment in Wisconsin than even we have suspected, or the pro-McCarthy, anti-Eisenhower boys wouldn't work themselves up into such a lather over our next recall effort.

"The hammy Sauk County cast reminds us of the seven-man troupe which used to play all fourteen parts of the Saturday-night melodrama at the Opera House back in the old home town in Iowa when we were a kid.

"In Act 1 the Sauk County cast strikes a pose as the phony and pious angels' chorus which bleats 'Praise the Lord' every time McCarthy gallops across the stage, wearing a tarnished brass halo which rattles like mad as he bows his bald pate. In the second act they double in corny jokes, and sell popcorn down the aisles. Just before the final curtain they get real nasty, rushing out from the wings to simultaneously stab the ingenue in her palpitating back.

"Starring in the Sauk County cast are GOP Committeeman Henry Ringling and County Chairman Bill Benzies, who confuse Senator McCarthy with the Almighty; Jack Rouse, GOP executive secretary, who sometimes confuses himself with Saint Peter at the pearly gates, where he makes sure that no Democrats enter without proper FBI clearance; and District Attorney Harlan Kelley, who is just confused.

"If an annoyed and highly unentertained customer rises to demand his money back, these jolly boys point a derisive finger at him and bleat in unison: 'He's trying to ruin our act.' Obviously, the act was ruined by the script writers, not the properly complaining customers.

"Kelley told the press Wednesday that he would issue warrants on some or all of five charges. He also warned in no uncertain terms that The Sauk-Prairie Star is a 'left wing' publication, which clearly demonstrates that Kelley's sense of direction is as faulty as his sense of propriety. We are, we confess, a couple of degrees to the left of Colonel McCormick of the Chicago Tribune. Kelley, apparently, is a little to the Colonel's right.

"County Chairman Bill Benzies' role was to help pack the state Republican convention with leather-lunged McCarthy fanatics, equipped to boo down any attempt to picture the junior senator as anything less than a Grade-A homogenized saint. In the performance of this role he short-circuited the voluntary committee and named the full slate of Door for Gore officers—those sturdy 200 per cent Americans dedicated to the virtuous Ku Klux Klan purpose of driving a fellow citizen out of his home town. But in spite of a convention carefully packed with McCarthy disciples, the top brass is still bewildered over the obvious fact that at least 25 per cent of the delegates were anti-McCarthy. Theirs is the embarrassing situation of the proud papa who does Junior's homework for him, and then gets mad as all get out because Junior's marks are so poor.

"Jack Rouse is busy stooping over looking under beds for circulators and signers to persecute and prosecute. Jack is a great hand for stooping over and looking under beds. Considering the grave danger of getting pushed flat on his puss, you'd think Jack would prefer an upright position, but uprightness has gone out of style since Joe began insisting you gotta smell like a skunk to be an effective politician.

"Mr. Ringling's role in this spectacular melodrama is strictly that of counting the gate receipts, as you might suspect of one descended from a long line of distinguished circus ancestors. Mr. Ringling hints that he has personally interviewed 2,200,000 electors of the state and found only 50,000 who confess to signing an anti-Joe petition. Considering the threats of Sing

Sing against those who circulate and sign, it's amazing that
Henry found fifty people in Wisconsin willing to stand up and
be counted among the more than a third of a million whose
signatures were legally notarized during the sixty-day recall
period. That he found 50,000 is phenomenal, and a great tribute to the courage of a great many people in Wisconsin."

Like I said, when you get involved in a recall movement
you wonder sometimes if you've suddenly developed holes
in your head. Kelley said vamoosing from the state was
melodrama. That it was. He said it was melodrama de-
signed solely to get me another headline. It wasn't. Here's
how I put it in the *Star:*

WE'RE TIRED OF PLAYING LITTLE EVA

"Last week the Wisconsin *State Journal* compared our whisk-
ing the McCarthy Recall Petitions out of the state with the
chilblain exploits of Little Eva hopping nimbly across the ice
a generation ago.

"Frankly, riding a North Central Airlines plane to Chicago
with the petitions safely stored in the luggage compartment,
we felt just about as silly as Little Eva looked on the stage of
the Gem Theatre at Exira, Iowa, where we last viewed Eva
some thirty-nine years ago. All the script lacked was a pack of
air-minded, baying bloodhounds hovering over the rudder of
the DC-3. District Attorney Harlan Kelley realistically played
the role of Simon Legree, complete with snarls and sneers.

"The Sauk County district attorney is apparently determined
to make a hero and a martyr out of us, even though we
haven't the slightest taste or talent for the role. All we've ever
asked was a chance to run an orderly country newspaper and
an orderly recall campaign. After three hectic months we could

use some peace and quiet; maybe a chance to play a few rounds of golf and watch TV, sans our silly puss. But Kelley, painfully possessed with the reincarnated melodramatic soul of the late Harriet Beecher Stowe, keeps casting us in heavy and burdensome roles as the frustrated hero with Villain Kelley panting passionately down our neck. You'd think Kelley would cast himself in a less sardonic and more sympathetic role, since he's writing the script, but every man to his taste.

"This historic Wednesday morning Kelley has summoned us before Justice Terbilcox at Baraboo to subpoena the third of a million anti-McCarthy signatures on recall petitions. Kelley knows he won't get the signatures. We've told him so often enough. What Kelley plans to do after that we haven't the faintest idea. We wouldn't be greatly surprised if he carried out his veiled threat and tossed us in the county clink for contempt. We wouldn't be surprised if he got a firm hold on his good judgment for a change and dismissed the charges. Nothing Kelley does surprises us any more. Script Writer Kelley is a great hand for what imaginative authors called 'The O. Henry Twist.'

"Our reasons for taking the petitions out of the state are the very simple reasons of a simple soul, and have nothing at all to do with melodrama. Kelley had threatened privately to seize them. We'd promised a third of a million people they wouldn't be seized. It's our conviction that Kelley has no legal or moral grounds to seize them. It seemed fundamental to us to move them across the state border where he couldn't seize them. If there's any melodrama in that situation, the melodrama is of Kelley's making, not ours.

"If Kelley followed his customary pattern, this is what would happen to the petitions once they got into his hands:

1. He'd hound and harass the signers and circulators, as Jack
    Rouse hinted in his Milwaukee speech a couple of weeks
    ago, to the end that signers and circulators wouldn't par-
    ticipate in the next recall effort;
2. He'd withhold the petitions from us, and perhaps misplace
    a substantial number of them, so we could make no use of
    the names in the next recall effort.

"At this moment names of signers and circulators on those
petitions are being checked for legality and carefully copied
so the same electors may be contacted when the recall effort is
relaunched. Interference with the recall process is specifically
denied Kelley or anyone else in the Wisconsin constitution.

"An accurate count of legal signatures and an accurate accounting of every penny collected by the Joe Must Go Club
will be made public. But the count and the accounting will
not be made by Kelley. If it took Kelley two months to examine our financial records, it would take him at least fifty
years to examine the names of a third of a million petition
signers. The county board raised enough of a ruckus over Kelley's expensive financial bill for the examination of our contributors. His financial bill for examining the petitions would
bankrupt the county.

"The count and the accounting of recall activities will be
made by officials properly authorized and equipped to render
an honest report.

"It's our urgent recommendation that Kelley stick to the
writing of melodrama, where his greatest genius lies."

Then it happened. Kelley subpoenaed the petitions.

This was not his sharpest piece of political strategy. I'd
said often enough and firmly enough that I'd go to jail
before I'd turn them over. Kelley must have known he'd

have to call my bluff, and he must have known he couldn't call my bluff.

Practically all of my friends were delighted at the prospect of me going to jail. So were two television networks, all the press services, the daily newspapers, and one national picture magazine. The National Press Photographers could have held a legal convention in the halls of the Sauk County courthouse that afternoon.

I left my pajamas and my toothbrush at home. I was probably the only occupant of the courthouse who figured that Kelley was kidding. Kelley is a great kidder.

"I'm not going to put him in jail," Kelley said dramatically. "I'm not going to make a martyr out of him."

I looked over my array of friends, and they were registering nothing but disgust and disappointment. Fine friends I have!

The post-recall era was not without its social embellishments. The "Victory in Defeat" party for local workers was held at the farm home of John and Doris Gasser. It was quite an affair. Ed Sachs, a fugitive from the stone-and-brick canyons of Chicago, kept wandering around the lawn pointing at the beautiful spruce trees. "How do they keep 'em so fresh so long after Christmas?" he marveled.

We urged Sachs to take a deep breath of invigorating, pine-scented air.

"I just learned to breathe when I came out here two months ago," he protested indignantly. "There's no point in overdoing it."

The Gasser kitchen was adorned with a portrait of me,

done by the competent hostess. For once I didn't look like a Methodist. More like a bruised and battered but unyielding Holy Roller.

There was one minor tragedy. Sachs fell off the piano bench late in the evening and sprained his shoulder.

The Republican state convention at Milwaukee was the strangest in Wisconsin history. I've attended lots of them. I've never witnessed anything like this. The state pro-McCarthy, anti-Eisenhower brass arranged for a packed hall. The only time the hall was filled was during Joe's speech. They filled the hall then by the simple device of dragging unsuspecting spectators off the streets to occupy the abundance of empty seats.

Harold Michael, president of the Joe Must Go Club, was heartily booed when he called on his party to repudiate McCarthy and support the President. But impartial observers estimated that 25 per cent of the crowd was silent in its approval.

The remarkable thing about all this is that the convention was, apparently, deliberately packed by the anti-Eisenhower, pro-McCarthy leaders of the state.

The jittery Republican county command refused to trust the voluntary GOP meeting. The delegates were hand picked by the "executive committee." The delegate list was topheavy with officers of the Door for Gore Club. Leading Eisenhower Republicans were left on the side lines, or appointed as alternates.

There were rumors of similar shenanigans all over the state. In Polk County, where Harold Michael is county

GOP chairman, there was a quiet attempt to pack the county meeting and oust him. But word gets around in the smaller communities. Michael suspected, and did a little packing of his own.

When the pro-McCarthy forces saw they were out-numbered, they called Michael aside and urged him not to make the recall a convention issue. Michael agreed, for the good of the party.

"But I remind you," he said, "that you *would* make the recall an issue if you had succeeded in packing the convention."

It was obvious that the anti-Eisenhower leaders couldn't find enough pro-McCarthy fanatics in Wisconsin to successfully pack their convention. It must have been very discouraging.

Kelley got me out of bed one night at 1 A.M. I don't remember what he said, but it was loud, and it wasn't complimentary.

"Why," I wanted to know "did you have to call me at this unholy hour? Anything you've said could have waited until morning."

"The United Press called me out of bed," he retorted.

"Do you have to make all your constituents unhappy merely because you're unhappy?" I wailed.

Meantime, Kelley's woes were piling up almost as rapidly as McCarthy's. He filed three "criminal informations" against three Milwaukee corporations which, he said, had donated money to us in violation of the Wisconsin corrupt-practices act. One of the three immediately protested. The wife of an officer had made the contribution. Kelley hadn't bothered to investigate. Frightened, he issued a public apology. Fortunately, the corporation officers were broadminded. They agreed not to seek damages.

John Semrad, a Sauk City resident who reassesses villages and cities of the state, urged the county board to withdraw Kelley's funds for investigating the Joe Must Go Club before he "bankrupted" the county, and "made the county the laughing stock of the state." Semrad was speedily joined by a LaValle resident, a Baraboo resident, and the Sauk County organized labor group. They charged:

1. That Kelley was investigating a state-wide movement with the tax funds of one small county. If an investigation were indicated, Kelley should turn his information over to the attorney general so the expense could be distributed over the state, and adequate facilities would be available for proper and thorough investigation.

2. That Kelley had taken on an impossible task. Semrad estimated Kelley would require fifty-five years.

3. That if one of three cases backfired, the county couldn't hope to avert damage actions for long. If Kelley served "a large number of warrants against a large number of people," the county might indeed be bankrupt.

At Milwaukee I tangled with Roman Reuter on Dave Garroway's question-and-answer TV show. It was quite an experience. This was the first color broadcast originating in Wisconsin. Mr. Garroway asked the questions from New York, relayed to us by earphone. The show was staged three times—once for the eastern audience early in the morning, a second time for the eastern-midwestern audience, and the last time for the midwestern-western audience. Mr. Reuter's most revealing statement was that the purpose of the Door for Gore Club was to "get Gore and his movement out of town," even though he had been telling the home-town people he solicited to sign his petition that he aimed only at the recall movement.

Mr. Reuter was quite insistent that I produce the third of a million petition signers of recall petitions on moral grounds, even though he recognized no moral obligation to produce the 400 signers he said he had on a petition to oust me.

To Reuter and some of his followers the two movements were parallel: I was trying to get McCarthy out of the Senate; they were trying to get me out of Sauk City.

I was especially pleased to speak at Tiffin, Ohio, where the Evangelical and Reformed Church was holding a conference on social problems. It was an excellent, constructive conference. There was, however, one embarrassing complication, resulting from the traditional failure of the clergy and the press to understand each other.

I had conveyed to the conference my fear that mccarthyism might swallow up all other news of the event. They were willing to take that chance.

Tiffin is a lovely town. A kind-hearted pastor agreed to meet me at the airport in Toledo. A reporter from the

Toledo *Blade* also met me. The reporter wanted an interview. The pastor had been instructed by the committee to speak to no one until the committee had consulted with me. I saw complications developing. Timidly, I made a suggestion. I had a carbon copy of my manuscript. Why not let the reporter have it, with instructions that he was not to release it until we telephoned permission?

Ministers and a great many other people do not understand the peculiar code of the press. A newspaper reporter may have the habits of a South Sea Island beachcomber and the morals of a second-story worker, but he will not, on threat of being burned at the stake, be persuaded to give up information which he has promised to keep secret.

We didn't make a deal. I attended a few of the convention sessions, and I regretted my inability to attend more. It was a sincere attempt to translate religion into everyday living.

But the big news of the convention, as I anticipated, was a three-column headline on page 1 of the Toledo *Blade* that the ministry wouldn't let me make a statement. It read something like a repetition of the Lindbergh kidnaping.

I wish schools of journalism would add a course in how to understand ministers, and theological schools would initiate a course in how to understand the press.

Back home Carl Lachmund and I sought an audience with Governor Walter Kohler. The request got speedy action. My telegram was delivered at 8:30 A.M. The governor's secretary telephoned that we could invade the governor's office at one-thirty that afternoon.

The room was comfortably filled with cameramen and reporters. The governor, one of the most handsome leaders in Wisconsin political history, was very pleasant. We protested that the John Doe inquiry could exhaust our finances and plague us forever without proving anything. We asked two things of the governor:

1. That he appoint a special governor's commission to thoroughly investigate our movement, and either prosecute or clear us.

2. That the governor recommend to the legislature revision in the antiquated John Doe statutes, apparently drafted in the early days when populations were scattered and the district attorney needed broad powers: (a) That public affairs be investigated publicly so that the principals would have an opportunity for counsel, and an opportunity to defend themselves; (b) That the district attorney be required to keep secret the names of parties involved in secret investigations under penalty of the law.

A representative from the attorney general's office was present. His chief contribution to the conversation was that we "hire a good lawyer." After several repetitions of this noble theme we were impressed with Ed Sachs's observation that maybe the attorney general's office was launching a new Association for Indigent Lawyers.

We were never able to convince the deputy attorney general that there is a considerable difference between professional politicians and ordinary citizens trying to do their civic duty as they saw it without hope of political reward.

All that came out of the conference was the governor's promise to telephone Mr. Kelley right away and urge that he speed up the investigation. This the governor did, but the only visible effect on Mr. Kelley was to make him as mad as the wayward spouse whose wife and mistress have been swapping notes on how loud he snores.

I doubt if I will be around fifty years from now, but if I am around and Kelley is around, the John Doe inquiry of the Joe Must Go Club will probably still be in progress unless someone with more ingenuity than we possess or more determination than the governor possesses manages to stop it.

The Kelley-Reuter combination can and probably will force me out of the newspaper business here. Small-town newspapers can't afford to lose many customers because there aren't many customers available. Neither can a modestly financed rural publisher endure expensive and endless litigation. But this is unimportant, and has nothing at all to do with the fate of mccarthyism.

It has a great deal to do with the need for legislative reforms in my state and probably in your state. Any law that permits a public official to use his investigative powers to persecute rather than to protect is a bad law.

Mr. Reuter—of all people!—demanded an apology, and I complied, after a fashion. Here's how:

Romie Reuter telephoned, demanding an apology for our intimation that the name of his mink ranch had been changed from Red Star to Gold Star. He says his ranch was never the Red Star. Apparently either our memory or our astigmatism has played us false. But Romie's excited refusal to be identified with anything red illustrates better than our sermon the ridiculous situation in which our fears have involved us. It would be as silly for George Wiedenfeld to change the name of his firm from the widely advertised and highly respected Red Star Dairy Equipment Co. to Green Star or Purple Star as it would be for Moscow Mills, Missouri or Moscow, Ohio, to suddenly and foolishly become Anti-Moscow Mills, Missouri, or Anti-Moscow, Ohio. If this shuddering fear of anything red gets much worse, thanks to the hysteria of mccarthyism, pretty soon we'll go around whispering "Isn't that a pretty ps-s-t sunset?" . . . We'll be singing "The ps-s-t, ps-s-t robin goes bob, bob, bobbin." "Hooray for the ps-s-t, white, and blue" . . . The horticulturists will have to do something about the color of red raspberries, red cherries, red cranberries, and red apples . . . Medical science may have to inject a green pigment into our blood streams lest we be accused of harboring Communistic corpuscles, and a guy with a red nose in January, or a gal with a red suntan in August will be brought before McCarthy's committee as a dangerous subversive . . . When mccarthyism not only repeals amendments to the Constitution of the United States, but begins to change the color scheme of nature and mankind, we wonder how silly the human race can get.

While the Republicans were juggling our problems like a hot potato, the Democrats recognized in these problems an effective campaign issue. Probably never before in all the history of Wisconsin have two Republicans been defended as vigorously as Carl Lachmund and I were defended by the Democrats. Gubernatorial candidate William Proxmire spoke openly and often, beseeching fair treatment for the recall participants, regardless of political faith.

From the Democratic convention floor Senator Henry Maier struck lustily and eloquently at Kelley and at the governor for his failure to discipline Kelley.

The Republicans said nothing, other than Kelley's oft-repeated statement that he was planning his every move with Attorney-General Verne Thompson, and Thompson's oft-repeated statement that he wasn't doing any such thing.

Wisconsin's only officially announced 100-per-cent McCarthy candidate, Ralph F. Amoth of Madison, withdrew from the gubernatorial race in these words from his office:

"Amoth cannot get enough signers to become a candidate for Republican governor due to his stand of backing McCarthy on his fight on Communists. Throughout Wisconsin, never have people of all faiths and religions shown such hatred, disgust, prejudice toward one man as they show toward Senator Joseph McCarthy."

Amoth sent nomination papers to thirty-six counties for circulation and only two were returned. His papers being circulated by seventy-six persons were returned with the same answer—that the people wouldn't sign because "Amoth was backing McCarthy."

He said the factions lining up against McCarthy include farmers, laborers, businessmen, housewives, the REA, and cooperatives. He said the initial recall movement hurt McCarthy and that the Wisconsin junior senator is "losing ground at a terrific rate in the southern half of Wisconsin on a straight line from LaCrosse to Lake Michigan." He declared "any candidate backing McCarthy is in for defeat," and that the people throughout the state are discussing McCarthy's record from the time he was a Democrat through his career as a circuit judge and his most recent activities during the televised Army-McCarthy hearings.

Included in these discussions, Amoth declared, are McCarthy's $10,000 Lustron deal, his record as a Marine Corps officer, his race for the Senate while he was still a Wisconsin circuit judge, his lack of proof to support many of his Communist charges, and his poor farm voting record.

He said: "Louis Bean, U.S. Department of Agriculture statistician, is correct in stating that McCarthy's strength is much overrated."

In spite of all this Amoth made it clear that he is "still for McCarthy." He favored McCarthy "hitting above the belt or below the belt to rid the state and country of Communists."

Kelley filed a **twenty-one-count** "information" against the Joe Must **Go Club** of Wisconsin, Inc., on novel grounds. It is illegal, he said, for a Wisconsin corporation to contribute money for political purposes. It was illegal, he said, for the corporation to pay nine persons, ten local Joe Must Go chapters, and two advertising agencies to promote the recall.

He also filed a motion in circuit court to hold me in contempt for failing to produce the recall petitions, even though less than 1 per cent of the signatures were secured in his jurisdiction, and even though they had never been presented for action.

The elephant had labored and begat an ant.

The vacation season was at hand in Wisconsin. Dozens of recall workers, circulators, and officers wanted to know if it would be safe for them to take a business or vacation trip—or if they might be summoned home by a Kelley subpoena.

I wired Kelley, requesting a public conference with the recall people to discuss this situation and his plans for the future. I also offered to move the recall offices to Baraboo temporarily in order to expedite Kelley's investigation.

Kelley called it a publicity gag. Anything that Kelley doesn't think of is a publicity gag, apparently.

Obviously, the McCarthy star is setting, and the Wisconsin recall organizations propose to speed the twilight.

Following the November election, a second recall effort will be launched, obviously predestined to success. Meantime, the Joe Must Go Club proposes to raise $50,000 to finance that recall, and to secure several million names from many states on a national recall petition. These names will be a dramatic demonstration to the Wisconsin electors that they have plenty of company in their disillusionment. But, more than that, they will serve a thoroughly practical purpose after the successful recall election has succeeded. Presented to the United States Senate, we are hopeful that they will effectively persuade that body that the ouster of McCarthy and the seating of his successor is a consummation devoutly desired not only by Wisconsin, but by the nation.

In one broad swoop the people of America can destroy not only mccarthyism but every other Evil Ism that feeds upon bigotry and hate . . . they can destroy the Evil Isms through this generation and a generation to come.

A nation free from the fears inspired by mccarthyism will fight Communism far more effectively than a nation divided. No matter what mccarthyism may tell you, the choice today is not between Communism and mccarthyism. Either of these choices will sabotage our liberties and fill our hearts with hate. The clear and unmistakable choice for all of us is a free and unfettered democracy in which free men shall exercise their freedoms unafraid.

America is ready to make that choice.

THE

McCARTHY PRIMER

Joe McCarthy was born under a lucky political star. His amazing, unbelievable political career has embraced a dozen spectacular scandals, any one of which would have wrecked any other politician.

McCarthy's secret has been the technique of attack—his fabulous ability to make the public forget a shoddy and unproductive past and present with the promise of an exciting, fruitful future. Mccarthyism is like the merry-go-round which tempts you aboard with gay and noisy promises of romance, but invariably lets you off exactly where you started.

Not once but many times McCarthy has used this successful technique. Never, until very recently, has he been forced on the defensive.

As a lawmaker, he has authored no important legislation. As a Communist hunter, he has caught no Communists. As a presumably gifted vote getter, he trailed his ticket in 1952. How McCarthy has created the illusion of magnificent achievement out of thin air is a phenomenon that will keep the students of political science busy for generations to come.

As a judge, McCarthy was chiefly famed for "quickie" divorces granted to political friends, and for the destruction of evidence in an important legal case.

As a Marine, he grossly exaggerated his war record for political purposes.

As a citizen, he ducked income-tax payments in his home state.

As a senator, he accepted a $10,000 manuscript fee from one firm and a substantial loan from the representative of another while he was promoting legislation helpful to these firms.

He has been trapped in dozen of deceits, and he has turned these deceits into virtues.

Yes, any one of these would have ruined a lesser politician. They have not ruined Joe McCarthy. He stands alone in American political history.

The public is asking hundreds of questions about this highly controversial figure and the recall movement. A few of the more frequent questions are answered on the following pages.

Q. Doesn't the recall movement aid communism because it seeks to remove from office the man who has led the fight against communism?

A. This question makes two basic assumptions: 1. That the McCarthy approach to the problem of communism is the only effective approach; 2. That Senator McCarthy is the only qualified leader of the fight against communism. Both are erroneous.

The fallacy of the McCarthy approach is evident in the record. He has caught no Communists. His committee has produced no effective anti-communist legislation. The committee, in fact, has produced only headlines for Senator Mc-Carthy.

Senator McCarthy's qualifications to fight communism are of an equally dubious nature. There is no evidence that the senator had even the slightest interest in the problem of communism previous to his Wheeling, West Virginia, speech on February 9, 1950—four and one-half years ago. Seven years of apprenticeship are required in the printing industry; it takes eight years to make a plumber. Senator McCarthy strains our credulity considerably when he expects us to believe that he has mastered the complex field of communism better than any living man with approximately half the experience required by the printing and plumbing trades.

Q.   Do you feel that the recall movement is an anti-Catholic manifestation?

A.   Bishop Sheil has frequently answered this question in language far more effective than mine. I recall the religious bigotry once aimed at Al Smith during his campaign for the presidency. I can understand how this bigotry has left an understandably bitter taste in the mouths of many a Catholic, and many Protestants, too. But thoughtful Catholics do not feel that the proper way to correct this political wrong is by yielding to the same political bigotry. My home town, for instance, is predominately Catholic. It is also predominately anti-McCarthy.

It rejected mccarthyism in the 1952 election. The absurd assumption that Catholics generally support mccarthyism for no better reason than that Senator McCarthy is a member of their faith is one I resent, and I'm sure it is resented by good Catholics everywhere.

Q.   Where can I best read the record of mccarthyism?

A.   Several excellent books have been written on the subject of McCarthy and mccarthyism. The most complete factual record has been produced by The Progressive, Madison 3, Wisconsin. Copies of this comprehensive, 92-page report are available at 75 cents each. An illuminating 68-page report titled *The Fort Monmouth Security Investigations* has been prepared by The Scientists' Committee on Loyalty and Security. This mimeographed report is available at 50 cents per copy from the Federation of American Scientists, 1749 L St., N. W., Washington 6, D.C.

Q.   Have you profited financially by the recall movement?

A.   I have devoted considerably less than one day a week to my small newspaper publishing business since I urged the recall last March. The recall has consumed practically all my time. I have neither asked nor received compensation for the time I have spent in recall activities. Due to my absence, my business has suffered a substantial loss in revenues. I have been reimbursed for some of my traveling expenses. These payments were detailed in a public statement released to the press some months ago. Copies of the complete financial report are available from the recall headquarters.

Q. What has the recall movement done to you personally?

A. Aside from the considerable financial burden, it has necessitated certain unpleasant family readjustments. It has
been necessary to send our eight-year-old daughter away
from home for the duration of the recall. The viciousness
of the pro-McCarthy fanatics—many of them sane and
temperate people on all other subjects—has disturbed
me, but the number of fanatics has been considerably
less than I anticipated. I have emerged from this initial
experience with a feeling that the human race is much
better than most of us suspect.

Q. Have you lost any personal friends because of the recall
movement?

A. A few. On the other hand, I have rediscovered many
friends out of my past.

Q. What is the most damning indictment against mccarthyism?

A. Intellectual stagnation. The greatness of America has
been built upon an open mind—a genius for flexibility—a
disposition to cull good ideas from many conflicting cul-
tures. Fanatical mccarthyism says we must build an
intellectual fence around America. Fanatical anti-mccarthyism says the same thing. Both are bad because they
make it a sin to study the political philosophies contrary
to ours. The lips of some teachers, and even some preachers, have been partially sealed by the dense intellectual
fog in many areas of "political science." Whatever its
virtues, it would be difficult to deny that mccarthyism has
largely created this fog. It is almost impossible to find an

honest factual account in the magazines or the newspapers of what communistic nations are doing. Part of this lack of information is due to the "Iron Curtain"; much of it is due to our fanatical prejudices. Writers fear to write such an account, publishers fear to publish it, and readers fear to read it. Nobody explains how we are effectively to fight the enemies of democracy if we know practically nothing about them. In my home town a few months ago fluoridation of drinking water was defeated by the bizarre warning that the Communists would poison us with fluorides. This absurdity scarcely requires any further comment.

Q. You were called a "political panhandler" and charged with running a "financial racket." If these statements aren't true, why don't you sue?

A. The newspaper reading public loves private lawsuits. Once I sued, I would become the issue rather than mccarthyism. There has already been too much of a tendency to make the recall appear as a private feud between me and McCarthy.

Q. Some people say the only reason you don't support McCarthy is because he didn't do anything for the dairy farmers. If this is true, then aren't you just a member of a pressure group?

A. Wisconsin is the No. 1 dairy state of the union. I have regretted and resented Senator McCarthy's neglect of the dairy industry, but no more than I have regretted and resented his neglect of other legislative problems, including the problem of anti-communist legislation. During his eight years in the Senate, I know of not one piece of constructive legislation with which he has been identified. Near the close of the last session he was one of three senators to vote for the ridiculous "firecracker" bill which proposed to legalize the shipment of firecrackers into states where their sale was prohibited. He was one of seven voting for Senator Malone's bizarre, dangerous proposal to convert foreign aids into airplanes, with eighty-one senators dissenting. He well deserves the title of "the nation's worst senator" conferred upon him by the working press.

Q. Senator McCarthy is a "specialist" in anti-communism. Isn't it unfair to expect him to be a specialist in other senatorial fields?

A. If Senator McCarthy were creating a great and enduring technique in communist opposition, a great many of us might be convinced. But even McCarthy's defenders are as vague about his technique as they are about his achievements. Senator LaFollette left us with a well-defined pattern of social achievement. Senator Vandenburg left us with a similarly well-defined pattern of international relations. Senator McCarthy will leave us with no pattern, no enduring achievement—nothing but a frustrated, post-Houdini feeling that we have been fooled into seeing things which aren't there at all.

Q. Fulton Lewis, Jr., has been particularly venomous in his attacks upon you. He has hinted that you are guilty of embezzlement. He has made other serious charges. Have these charges hurt you, are they honest charges, and if not why has he been so vicious?

A. For a reporter with a national reputation Mr. Lewis has shown an amazing disregard for the truth. His violent attacks have doubtless discouraged some timid contributors, which was his obvious purpose. But for the most part they have cheered me considerably. Mr. Lewis' close association with the leaders of mccarthyism is no secret. Obviously, he reflects the thinking of this leadership. Just as obviously, Mr. Lewis' hymn of hate is motivated by the gripping fear that the next recall will succeed. I only wish that those opposed to McCarthy were as certain of our success as Mr. Lewis and those who favor McCarthy.

Q. Mr. Lewis described you as "not particularly bright" on one of his broadcasts. What's your comment?

A. We'd been trying to keep the state of my intellect a secret. After those in the Mutual studio at Washington generally conceded that Fulton and I came out about even in our fifteen-minute bout, it didn't occur to me that he would be the one to betray my secret.

Q. Are you against senatorial investigations of such subjects as communism, graft, and corruption?

A. No. Effective investigations of these subjects have often been helpful to our governing processes. But the pretense that these investigations must sink to a low level of deceit and sensationalism, and that the junior senator from Wisconsin is the only man in the Senate capable of conducting such an investigation is more than a little ridiculous.

Q. How do you explain a state like Wisconsin with a liberal background producing a senator like McCarthy?

A. In 1946 McCarthy was a liberal, recently migrated from the Democratic party to the GOP. The real contest was in the primary. He won by a scant margin of 5,387 votes over Robert M. LaFollette, Jr., by two devices: 1. The exploitation of "Tail Gunner Joe's" war record, and 2. An expensive and extensive publicity campaign financed by the then communist-dominated Wisconsin CIO which vigorously opposed LaFollette. McCarthy said nothing to discourage this support. When chided about it he did say: "Communists have as much right to vote as anyone, haven't they?" In 1952 McCarthy rode into office on Eisenhower's coattails. He trailed the Republican ticket in the general election, winning by 139,042 votes, compared with Eisenhower's margin of 357,569, Governor Kohler's margin of 407,327, and Secretary of State Fred Zimmerman's margin of 505,300. Zimmerman has long been an outspoken foe of McCarthy, and McCarthy attempted to purge him in the primary. Had it not been for Ike's tremendous popularity and the desire of the Eisenhower Republicans to give President Ike a Republican senator, it is fairly obvious that McCarthy would have been defeated. Since November 1952 Eisenhower Republicans have been permanently and angrily disillusioned. Today, McCarthy's support comes from two sources: The relatively small group of fanatics who will always support him; and the disgruntled wing of the Taft faction which still hopes to play the 1952 convention over again and bring Taft back to life. If Taft were alive today, I suspect that he would be among the severe critics of mccarthyism, but without his leadership some of his friends in the party have taken the bizarre position that mccarthyism is more important than Republicanism.

Q. Do you think McCarthy's ambition is to be president?

A. There is no ceiling over McCarthy's ambitions. He
switched party affiliations, presumably for selfish political
reasons, since he has shown no disposition for loyalty to
either party. He switched from a "liberal internationalist"
to a "conservative nationalist" presumably because he believed there was a better source of money and votes in
the latter camp. McCarthy became a shrewd political an-
alyst the hard way—through defeat. If he is convinced he
can win, he will try for the presidency. There are some
indications that he may be stronger nationally than he is
in Wisconsin. Outside of Wisconsin the anti-McCarthy
group is composed of those who regard him as a moral
problem. Inside Wisconsin there is just as great an em-
phasis recently on his pitiful legislative record. Many a
farmer, laborer, or businessman in Wisconsin has suddenly awakened to McCarthy's amazing betrayal of the
economic interests of the state. This awakening has been
expedited by the unfortunate drop in milk prices and ac-
companying industrial problems.

Q. Where would McCarthy turn if the recall were successful and he were ousted from the Senate?

A. It's a safe guess that he might spearhead some kind of a
well-financed, "right-wing" group predicated upon the
phony hunt for Communists, and a philosophy of nation-
alism. It's an equally safe guess that he would brand Wisconsin as a den of iniquity and subversion. Abetted by
Buckley, Lewis, Pegler, and the other slick tongues at his
disposal, he might make the cloak of martyrdom fit without alterations. But, stripped of senatorial immunity and
senatorial powers, his followers would soon tire of him.

Q. Is it true that most rich men back McCarthy? If so, why?

A. It is as dangerous and bigoted to make generalizations
about any economic group as it is to make generalizations about religious or racial groups. You may be sure
that the poor man who criticizes the rich man would be
in the rich man's shoes if he knew how to get there.
There is one safe generalization about a great many rich
men, however. They have a peculiar genius for making
money. Geniuses, whether they operate in the field of
economics or the atom bomb, are apt to possess a one-
track mind. Otherwise, they wouldn't be geniuses. Because
of this narrow and peculiar gift, the genius in any field
is apt to be a child in politics. The thinking of some rich
men of my acquaintance goes no further than the fear
that what they have may be taken away from them. They
are terrified by the mere mention of communism because
communism takes from the rich and gives to the poor,
presumably. They are annoyed by foreign aid because
they have a feeling that their tax monies are being
squandered by foreigners. They are "suckers" for an anti-
communist, nationalistic appeal.

Q. Are the "common people" likely to turn communistic in
this country if a crisis develops?

A. No. The peasants of Russia and China might turn natural-
ly to communism because their lot could scarcely be
worse than it has been under their former form of government. But in America there are no self-effacing
peasants. The worker on the production line may sit on
the city council, or be commander of the American
Legion. He might turn to a dictatorship which fits his

personal prejudices in a crisis, in the hope that he may
be somebody in the new scheme of things, but he won't
turn to a communistic philosophy which makes him a
nobody.

Q. Do the McCarthy fanatics in Wisconsin believe Mc-
Carthy's charge that General Marshall is guilty of treason?

A. Unfortunately, the fanatics believe everything McCarthy
tells them. On the other hand, there are the intellectuals
among the McCarthy disciples, like William Buckley,
Jr. who reject McCarthy's extravagances, but justify them
on an interesting basis. Mr. Buckley, for instance, admits
that Marshall is not a traitor, but it's quite all right, he
says, for McCarthy to call him a traitor because Marshall's
friends have exaggerated his virtues and McCarthy is
merely "cutting him down to size." This is the equivalent
of saying that if one of your neighbors seeking a job or
political office is overpraised, you should charge him with
smoking opium and robbing banks to "cut him down to
size." Obviously, this wouldn't cut him down to size at all.
It would merely brand him as an opium smoker, and a
bank robber, and you would probably have an embarrassing lawsuit on your hands if you had no senatorial
privilege.

Q. Are the people of Texas unanimously friends of Mc-
Carthy?

A. No. We receive numerous letters assuring us that "we
Texans don't want Joe either."

Q.   Do you want to be senator in McCarthy's place?

A.   No. I want to be an undistinguished, golf-playing country editor again. Television cameras and microphones
don't fascinate me. They terrify me. Besides, if I sought
public office I would immediately and effectively be
charged with launching the recall for this very purpose.

Q.   What's this about McCarthy once being a Democrat?

A.   In August 1936 he was elected president of the Young
Democratic Clubs of Wisconsin's Seventh District. In
November of that year he ran for the office of district
attorney of Shawano County on the Democratic ticket.
He was defeated, whereupon he switched political affilia-
tions.

Q.   What was McCarthy's history as a circuit judge?

A.   He was elected in 1939 and served on the bench four
years. Judge McCarthy first achieved fame of a sort by
the granting of "quickie" divorces to political friends and
supporters, apparently a device to build a political machine. Afterward, many of the divorce principals and their
attorneys were supporters of McCarthy's political ambitions, sometimes with cash. In 1940 Judge McCarthy was
in the headlines again when he dismissed a state charge
against an Appleton firm and ordered statements in the
record destroyed by the court reporter. The Wisconsin
Supreme Court unanimously found Judge McCarthy's
actions an abuse of judicial power, and criticized the
destruction of his notes in this language: "Ordering destruction of these notes was highly improper. We can only
say that if it were necessary to a decision, the destruction

of evidence under these circumstances could only be open to the inference that the evidence destroyed contained statements of fact contrary to the position taken by the person [McCarthy] destroying the evidence."—239 Wis. 258.

Q. Was McCarthy illegally elected to the United States Senate in 1946?

A. The Wisconsin Supreme Court said he was. McCarthy ran for the Senate, although his term as judge was not to expire until 1951, in violation of Section 10, Article VII of the Wisconsin Constitution: "Each of the judges of the Supreme and Circuit Courts . . . *shall hold no office of public trust* except a judicial office, during the term for which they are respectively elected and *all votes for either of them for any office, except a judicial office, given by the legislature or the people, shall be void.*"

In demanding disciplinary action against McCarthy, the State Board of Bar Commissioners declared in its petition to the Supreme Court that McCarthy was guilty of "violating the public policy of the State of Wisconsin, the Code of Judicial Ethics, his Oath of Office as a Judge, and his Oath of Office as a Member of the Bar." In even stronger language the Board said: "It is difficult to conceive of any conduct upon the part of a presiding judge which would bring judges into greater disrepute and contempt than the conduct of the defendant (McCarthy) challenged in this proceeding."

While the Supreme Court said its hands were tied because McCarthy held a federal rather than a state office, it did make this judgment of McCarthy's conduct: "Under the facts of this case, we can reach no other conclusion than that the defendant [McCarthy], by accepting and holding the office of United States Senator during the term for which he was elected Circuit Judge, did so in violation of the terms of the Constitution and laws of the State of Wisconsin, and in so doing violated his oath as Circuit Judge and as an attorney of law."—State v. McCarthy. 255 Wis. 234.

McCarthy angrily demanded the resignation of the entire board of Bar Commissioners, but no one took him seriously.

Q.   In view of this decision by the Supreme Court, isn't the recall a futile effort?

A.   No. The recall does not assume jurisdiction by the State Supreme Court. It assumes jurisdiction by the United States Senate, which would look very silly indeed contending that the people who elected a senator could not recall him, but the Senate which didn't elect him could impeach him.

Q.   What about McCarthy's war record?

A.   With the exception of his resignation, at a critical period in the fighting, to run for public office, it was no better or no worse than thousands of other American boys. It's the political exploitation of that record which has inspired widespread criticism of McCarthy.

Although his 1946 senatorial campaign hailed him as "Tail Gunner Joe," and boasted that he enlisted in the Marines as a private, neither is true. Joe never served a day as a private. He enlisted as an intelligence officer. He never qualified as a tail gunner, although he apparently flew some routine missions in that position as a gag after the enemy had been cleared out.

McCarthy denies a campaign statement he's reported to have made at Badger Village that he wore built-up shoes because he was "carrying shrapnel in my leg." But Badger Village is only a few miles from Sauk City and many of my neighbors heard that speech. They agree unanimously that he made the statement. Actually, Mc-Carthy was injured during a hazing ceremony while his ship was crossing the equator. Specifically, he's said to have fallen off a ladder with a bucket on his foot, and his foot was injured. McCarthy does *not* hold the Purple Heart, although a disgruntled Marine hero who had been in the thick of the fighting sent him his Purple Heart a few months ago with a blistering comment on Joe's claims to heroism.

Joe resigned from the Marines on December 11, 1944, three months before the bloody struggle for Iwo Jima, four months before the battle of Okinawa. He resigned to begin his campaign against Senator Robert M. LaFollette, Jr., with the exploitation of "Tail Gunner Joe's" service record.

Q. Is McCarthy a literary genius?

A. Apparently Lustron, a prefab housing corporation which ultimately went into a receivership after borrowing $37,-500,000 from the government, thought so. McCarthy sold them a $10,000 manuscript for a housing booklet back in 1948 when the Appleton Bank was pressing him for a reduction of his bank loan. If Shakespeare were alive today, he wouldn't command this kind of word rates.

Ever since Joe collected handsomely from Lustron his
critics have been suggesting that Joe's activities on the
Banking and Currency Committee, which did a great deal
for housing firms like Lustron, may have had more to do
with his $10,000 manuscript fee than his literary skill. As
Clyde M. Foraker, receiver for Lustron, who bluntly
called the McCarthy deal "unethical," said once: "I'll bet
he wouldn't have gotten the $10,000 if he hadn't been a
senator." That seems to be a fairly safe bet.

Q.   Is McCarthy a financial wizard?

A.   Apparently yes. McCarthy used Lustron's $10,000 literary
fee to buy Seaboard Airlines Railroad stock. Later he sold
1,000 shares of this stock at a profit of $35,614.75. After-
ward the senatorial committee investigating McCarthy
asked this pertinent question:

   "Was there any relationship between Senator Mc-
Carthy's position as a member of the Senate Banking and
Currency Committee and his receipt of confidential infor-
mation relating to the stock of the Seaboard Airlines
Railroad which was indebted to the RFC for sums in
excess of $15,000,000?"—Hennings Report, p. 18.

Q.   Where did McCarthy get the title "The Pepsi-Cola Kid"?

A.   In 1947 the Pepsi-Cola Company wanted more sugar to
increase its soft-drink output. McCarthy was carrying
the ball for them, loudly demanding the end of sugar
rationing. At the same time Russell M. Arundel, Pepsi-
Cola lobbyist, endorsed McCarthy's note for $20,000 to
relieve McCarthy of pressing financial obligations with
the Appleton bank.

Q. What were McCarthy's income-tax troubles?

A. One illustration: In 1944 McCarthy claimed exemption
from Wisconsin income tax on the grounds that he was
in the armed services outside the state and had received
no income from the state. He conveniently "forgot" to
mention a taxable income of $41,854.67 from sale of stocks
and from stock dividends. In 1947 the assessor of incomes
reminded him of this oversight. Meantime, of course,
McCarthy was glad to claim residence in Wisconsin
when he ran for public office. He ultimately paid a state
tax of $2,459.54 and $218.32 interest.

Q. Isn't it unfair to use any of the charges of misdeeds previous to 1952 against McCarthy, since the voters of Wisconsin passed judgment on him at that time?

A. No. Unfortunately, the press of Wisconsin was so generally and fanatically pro-McCarthy in 1952 that few
newspapers gave his misdeeds any publicity at all. Only
now are the people of Wisconsin beginning to find out
that mccarthyism is not a new development.

Q. Do you "hate" McCarthy?

A. No. Joe, unless he has changed lately, is a friendly, ex-
troverted soul. At the beginning of his phony anti-communist campaign the whole thing was a vaudeville act with
Joe. At the conclusion of an impassioned, rabble-rousing
speech, during the course of which he has called both the
Milwaukee *Journal* and the Madison *Cap-Times* "Wisconsin editions of the *Daily Worker*," I have been immensely amused to witness Joe leap from the stage, and

guilelessly inquire of the fuming members of the Mil-
waukee-Madison press: "How did I do tonight?" It is the
ambition of every clown, I've heard, to play Shakespeare,
and I fear that Joe has suddenly decided to play Shakespeare. It would be difficult, if not impossible, for one
who has known Joe to "hate" him. We can hate the things
he stands for, and still exempt Joe from our hate. Joe's
fanatical followers are much worse than Joe. I doubt if
Joe, at least until very recently, recognized the tragic consequences of his extravagances. To Joe it was a vaudeville
act; to his followers it is the gospel of their master. I am
frequently grieved at the tremendous waste of talent that
McCarthy represents. It would make me very happy
indeed if McCarthy could be persuaded to turn his remarkable talents into useful and constructive fields. It is
obvious, however, that this transformation of character
will not occur, unless McCarthy is sternly and unmistaka-
ably rebuked. Just as obviously, this stern rebuke can
come from only one source—the aroused electorate of the
sovereign state of Wisconsin.